D1565669

JEAN-PAUL SARTRE
Politics and Culture in Postwar France

Also by Michael Scriven

* SARTRE'S EXISTENTIAL BIOGRAPHIES

* PAUL NIZAN: COMMUNIST NOVELIST

EUROPEAN SOCIALIST REALISM

WAR AND SOCIETY IN TWENTIETH-CENTURY FRANCE

* SARTRE AND THE MEDIA

TELEVISION BROADCASTING IN CONTEMPORARY FRANCE AND BRITAIN

* *from the same publishers*

Jean-Paul Sartre

Politics and Culture in Postwar France

Michael Scriven
Professor of European Studies
University of the West of England, Bristol

First published in Great Britain 1999 by
MACMILLAN PRESS LTD
Houndmills, Basingstoke, Hampshire RG21 6XS and London
Companies and representatives throughout the world

A catalogue record for this book is available from the British Library.

ISBN 0–333–63321–0

First published in the United States of America 1999 by
ST. MARTIN'S PRESS, INC.,
Scholarly and Reference Division,
175 Fifth Avenue, New York, N.Y. 10010

ISBN 0–312–22194–0

Library of Congress Cataloging-in-Publication Data
Scriven, Michael, 1947–
Jean-Paul Sartre : politics and culture in Postwar France /
Michael Scriven.
p. cm.
Includes bibliographical references (p.) and index.
Other title: Politics and culture in Postwar France.
ISBN 0–312–22194–0 (cloth)
1. Sartre, Jean Paul, 1905– —Political and social views.
2. Politics and culture—France. I. Title. II. Title: Politics
and culture in Postwar France.
B2430.S34S369 1999
320'.092—dc21 98–55201
CIP

This book is printed on paper suitable for recycling and made from fully managed and sustained forest sources.

10 9 8 7 6 5 4 3 2 1
08 07 06 05 04 03 02 01 00 99

Printed and bound in Great Britain by
Antony Rowe Ltd, Chippenham, Wiltshire

In memory of Elizabeth Scott

'Knowledge which is not constantly criticised, transcending itself and reaffirming itself in the light of such criticism, has no value … The only way to learn is to protest.'

J.-P. Sartre, 1968

Contents

List of Abbreviations ix

Preface xi

Acknowledgements xv

1 Initial Thoughts 1

PART I SARTRE'S REVOLUTIONARY POLITICS

2 Sartrean Politics: Transition and Division 7

3 Sartre and de Gaulle: Two Conceptions of France 17

4 Sartre and the Nizan Affair: The Cold War Politics of French Communism 41

5 Sartre and the Politics of Violence: Maoism in the Aftermath of May 1968 63

PART II SARTRE'S CULTURAL POLITICS

6 Sartre and Commitment: Reinventing Cultural Forms 83

7 Myth versus Satire: The Dramatised Politics of Sartre's *Nekrassov* 97

8 Ideological Art Criticism: Sartre and Giacometti 113

9 Mediated Politics: Sartre and Chomsky Revisited 133

Postscript: A Final Word on Sartre 153

English Translation of the Principal Titles Cited in French 155

Notes and References 157

Bibliography 181

Index 189

List of Abbreviations

ORGANISATIONS

A2	Antenne 2
CNE	Comité National des Ecrivains
GATT	General Agreement on Tariffs and Trade
GP	Gauche Prolétarienne
NRP	Nouvelle Résistance Prolétarienne
ORTF	Organisation de la Radio-Télévision Française
PCF	Parti Communiste Français
PCI	Partito Communista Italiano
RDR	Rassemblement Démocratique Révolutionnaire
RPF	Rassemblement du Peuple Français
SFIO	Section Française de l'International Ouvrière
UDR	Union des Démocrates pour la République

TEXTS

The place of publication of all works cited is Paris unless otherwise indicated.

Works by Sartre

SIT1	*Situations I* (Gallimard, 1947)
SIT2	*Situations II* (Gallimard, 1948)
SIT3	*Situations III* (Gallimard, 1949)
SIT4	*Situations IV* (Gallimard, 1964)
SIT5	*Situations V* (Gallimard, 1964)
SIT6	*Situations VI* (Gallimard, 1964)
SIT7	*Situations* VII (Gallimard, 1965)
SIT8	*Situations* VIII (Gallimard, 1972)
SIT9	*Situations* IX (Gallimard, 1972)
SIT10	*Situations* X (Gallimard, 1976)
TDS	*Un théâtre de situations* (Gallimard, 1973)

Bibliographical Reference Texts

ES M. Contat and M. Rybalka, *Les Ecrits de Sartre* (Gallimard, 1970)

ES2 M. Contat and M. Rybalka, 'Les Ecrits de Sartre de 1969 à 1971', *Le Magazine Littéraire*, Nos 55–6, September 1971, pp. 36–41.

Preface

Sartre died in 1980. Twenty years later, at the dawn of the twenty-first century, Sartre's position as French intellectual icon, charismatic representative of a possibly historically dated species, appears somewhat dated, almost anachronistic. In today's technological society, the role of the traditional intellectual is limited, if not defunct. And yet, the popular appeal, the populist strand at the heart of Sartre's life and work, remain for me residually fascinating and admirable. The huge crowds of ordinary people who transformed his funeral into a gigantic act of celebration of the ideas and values that he symbolised testified to his social and cultural importance. This book, the third and last that I shall write on Sartre, is consequently my final attempt to explain why, in my view, Sartre remains important today.

Sartre was almost certainly the most widely studied writer and intellectual of the twentieth century. The thousands and thousands of references to Sartre's work in numerous languages listed in the most recent edition of the International Sartre Bibliography constitute ample proof of the assertion.[1] The sheer volume and range of Sartre's output is simply staggering: philosophy, political writings, literary criticism, fiction, drama, art criticism, biography, autobiography, film scripts, essays, journalism ... the list is almost endless. Every conceivable way of arranging words on paper was explored by Sartre during his lifetime. It is, however, not merely the quantitative aspect of his writings that is impressive (the final biography of Flaubert, alone, comprising approximately two million words, is a suitably gargantuan example); it is above all the originality and intellectual brilliance at the heart of his work that impresses. Two anecdotes will suffice to underline this brilliance.

The first relates to the conference on 'Postwar Paris: Art and Existentialism' held in 1993 at the Tate Gallery in

London.[2] Olivier Todd, although extremely hostile to Sartre's politics and even sceptical about Sartre's ability to understand anything whatsoever about painting and sculpture, had no reservations regarding Sartre's intellectual brilliance, his capacity to generate ideas spontaneously on any conceivable topic. He told the story of one of Sartre's numerous visits to art galleries in Italy. Sartre began at one point to voice aloud his ideas on the paintings in front of him, a brilliant disquisition on the relative merits of Tintoretto and Titian. Soon a crowd gathered around him to listen to what he had to say, and in no time at all there were approximately a hundred people following Sartre around the art gallery convinced that he was the official guide, so perceptive and informative did his ideas appear to be.

The second anecdote relates to an interview in 1961 between Sartre and the British critic, Kenneth Tynan. Tynan wanted to discover Sartre's views on the relationship between right-wing politics and the contemporary French theatre. Unfortunately, Tynan's spoken French was not quite up to the mark, and instead of asking Sartre a question about the political right (*la droite*), he in fact asked a question relating to the law and the legal system (*le droit*). The question that Tynan actually asked therefore had no bearing at all on anything that had preceded in the interview. Nonetheless, the response that Sartre gave was quite brilliant, a lengthy analysis of the legal foundation of contemporary French theatre. Tynan insisted on including the response in the published version of the interview that appeared in the *Observer* as a tribute to what he termed Sartre's 'mental agility'.[3]

It was neither Sartre's intellectual brilliance, nor his literary and philosophical originality, nor the voluminous quantity of his multi-faceted writings that prompted so many people to take to the streets of Paris on the day of his funeral, however. His popular appeal lay elsewhere. Sartre was one of those annoying people who held dissident views on just about everything that you could think of: the international world order, the political and economic organisation of contemporary society, especially France, the institutional and legal frameworks that regulate the lives of ordinary citizens, the educational system, the media networks that control and disseminate information. Sartre systematically refused to keep quiet about what he saw as inequalities and injustices in the world. He was prepared to sacrifice both institutional honours and financial rewards in order to speak his mind.

When I was first introduced to the work of Sartre in 1968, the impact on me was profound, not because of the bulk and intellectual scope of Sartre's writings (although even today I can remember my first encounter with *L'Etre et le neant* – a breathtaking moment of realisation that writing of such monumental proportions was possible); rather, it was the *exemplary* quality of Sartre's existence that struck me then, and remains with me even today at the turn of the century: an intellectual who throughout his life refused quite simply to be bought off by the Establishment. It is this, in my view, exemplary attitude that I shall seek to bring out in this book through an exploration of Sartre's involvement in the politics and culture of postwar France. It is this exemplary attitude that will, irrespective of changing intellectual fashions and whims, and of far-reaching social transformations, continue to remain topical and relevant well into the twenty-first century.

The full responsibility for the ideas expressed in the following pages is mine alone. I would, however, like to take this opportunity to thank a number of friends and colleagues who have been of great assistance to me in the production of this book. First, I would like to thank Olivier Todd for his generosity in sharing with me on numerous occasions his personal insights into the life and work of Sartre. Although ultimately I do not share Olivier's views, his unique Franco-British perspective on matters Sartrean has proved an invaluable sounding board against which to test my own ideas. Second, I wish to thank Michel Contat, whose extensive and detailed knowledge of Sartre's writings has provided me with a far better understanding of Sartre than would otherwise have been the case. I would also like to thank all colleagues, in particular Christina Howells, Jean-Pierre Boulé, Andrew Leak and Annette Lavers, who have worked with me to promote the cause of the UK Society for Sartrean Studies (UKSSS) and its journal, *Sartre Studies International*. The activities of both the Society and the journal since 1992 have provided me with countless memorable opportunities to deepen my understanding of Sartre's life and work in discussions with Sartrean specialists from Europe, North America and beyond. It is also appropriate for me to thank the British Academy, the Institute of Romance Studies and the Institut Français for their financial and material support for the annual conferences of UKSSS. In this respect, Olivier Poivre d'Arvor at the Institut Français has been extremely supportive of our endeavours. Finally, at a more practical level, I wish to thank Martyn Hoskins and Jeremy Fogg for their enduring patience in solving seemingly endless technical word-processing problems, and also Jessa Karki and Colleen McKean for all their support in producing the final typescript.

MICHAEL SCRIVEN

Acknowledgements

A version of Chapter 4 first appeared in *Sartre Studies International*, vol. 2, no. 1, 1996. A version of Chapter 7 first appeared in the *Journal of European Studies*, vol. xviii, 1988. I am grateful to the editors for permission to reprint.

All translations are my own unless otherwise indicated.

1

Initial Thoughts

To write a third book on Sartre might at first sight appear rash or at the very least unnecessary. There is nonetheless an underlying logic in such an enterprise. This, my last book on Sartre, is above all else an attempt to capture the defining characteristics of a life and a work that in my opinion set Sartre apart from other twentieth-century French writers and intellectuals. In my two previous books on Sartre, one centred on biography,[1] the other on the media,[2] I have alluded to this intrinsic differentiation at various points in my argument. The very title of this book, however, 'Politics and Culture in Postwar France', is designed to place what I consider to be the interconnected politico-cultural originality of Sartre's life and work at the centre of attention throughout. Somewhere at the intersection of the political and the cultural lies the enduring value of Sartre's writings. I have previously made a similar case for Nizan in the context of the 1930s.[3] In the context of postwar France Sartre's work embodies and synthesises a historical period in a manner which calls for special attention.

The structure and content of what follows are consequently predicated on the belief that in order to grasp Sartre's unique contribution to postwar French intellectual life it is necessary to focus as much on the nature of Sartre's insertion in the politics and political culture of the postwar period as on the manner in which this insertion shapes and is shaped by his writings and cultural interventions. It is precisely this process of interconnection between the political and the cultural which constitutes Sartre's exemplarity and originality in the postwar period, and which is at the root of a life-defining attitude to existence that will in my view continue to exercise a residual and seductive fascination over many readers for many years to come.

In order to elucidate the specific nature of Sartre's political and cultural orginality, a particular organisational and methodological approach would consequently appear to impose itself. There exist already a number of commendable studies of Sartre's political theory and political practice,[4] as well as countless publications on Sartre's cultural production.[5] In each of these works a particular facet of Sartre's output is analysed, with varying degrees of attention paid to the relative claims of theory and practice. What these texts do not seek to do, however, is to capture what I can best define as the underlying synthesising project that propels Sartre forward through the different stages of his life. The aim in this study, therefore, is to disclose the specific nature of Sartre's overarching politico-cultural project as it manifests itself at key moments in the postwar period from 1945 until his death in 1980.

Analysis will be divided into two parts, the first focused on Sartre's political activities (Part I: Sartre's Revolutionary Politics), the second on cultural affairs (Part II: Sartre's Cultural Politics). There will, however, be no attempt in either part to offer a comprehensive chronological overview of Sartre's politics or of Sartre's cultural production. Instead, attention will centre principally on key case-studies selected for detailed scrutiny precisely because they exemplify important illustrative components of Sartre's global politico-cultural project. This 'emblematic' case-study approach constitutes the basic methodological and organisational structure of what follows. In each of the two primary parts, an initial chapter will sketch out a preliminary political/cultural contextualisation. Subsequent chapters will examine in detail specific case-studies in order to highlight key features in Sartre's postwar intellectual itinerary and to build up progressively a composite picture of this multi-faceted Sartrean politico-cultural project.

Hence, in Part I ('Sartre's Revolutionary Politics'), an initial synoptic survey (Chapter 2) will elucidate Sartre's historical status as a postwar intellectual, focusing specifically on the nature of his insertion in French political culture and on his political and ideological itinerary between 1945 and 1980. Subsequent chapters in Part I will centre on Sartre's relations with the three key political movements of the time: Gaullism (Chapter 3), communism (Chapter 4) and Maoism (Chapter 5). Here, the objective will be to disclose the defining characteristics of Sartre's relationship with these three ideological movements through the critical lens of a particular issue that enables new insights to emerge: Sartrean and Gaullist conceptions of France in Chapter 3, the Cold War politics of French communism in Chapter 4, and the Maoist politics of violence in Chapter 5.

Likewise in Part II ('Sartre's Cultural Politics'), an initial critical survey (Chapter 6) will examine the overall problematic of Sartre's theory and practice of commitment as a prelude to a series of culturally-based case-studies. Given the range and extent of Sartre's cultural output, case-studies have been selected with a view to displaying the manner in which Sartre's political and ideological views find expression in as wide a range of cultural forms as possible: theatre, art criticism and the audiovisual media. Chapter 7 is accordingly centred on the dramatisation of politics in Sartre's openly satirical play, *Nekrassov*, Chapter 8 examines Sartre's ideological art criticism with specific reference to the work of Giacometti, and Chapter 9, written from a deliberately journalistic perspective, explores the mediation of Sartre's politics in the press and in newly emerging audiovisual cultural forms through juxtaposition and comparison with the ideas of Chomsky.

The overall ambition of *Jean-Paul Sartre: Politics and Culture in Postwar France* is to present Sartre as an exemplary figure in a complex and evolving post-1945 political and cultural landscape. The inner dynamism and originality of Sartre's work is located precisely in the tense relationship that he maintained throughout his life between deeply held revolutionary political beliefs and a residual yet critical attachment to traditional forms of cultural expression.

Like Nizan in the 1930s, the force of Sartre's writings resides above all else in the intermeshing of political convictions and cultural expression. In the post-1945 period, in particular, as Sartre's political stance became progressively more radical, the need to experiment with different forms of cultural expression became increasingly more urgent. The consequence was that Sartre's importance as a postwar intellectual figure is ultimately inextricably linked to this continual process of negotiation between radical political ideas and traditional cultural forms that are themselves challenged by the emerging culture of the audiovisual media. It is this process of deepening politicisation and broadening cultural experimentation which is at the heart of the analysis that follows and which constitutes the singular exemplarity of Jean-Paul Sartre.

Part I
Sartre's Revolutionary Politics

2

Sartrean Politics: Transition and Division

In an illuminating commentary on Sartre's intellectual itinerary, Jean-Bertrand Pontalis characterised Sartre's politics as a ceaseless quest for the agent in the historical process.[1] For Pontalis, Sartre's political evolution is best understood as an attempt to locate and engage with privileged agents of social change at different moments in Sartre's own ideological evolution. In practical terms this translated itself into a three-stage developmental process during which Sartre successively privileged first the individual, second the Communist Party, and third youth. In Pontalis's interpretative schema what remains paramount throughout is the systematic rejection by Sartre of all forms of philosophical and political passivity, and an ensuing commitment to focus on those key agencies whose historical agenda was actively to dislocate in some way or other the established order of things. Although perhaps slightly reductive in scope and complexity, Pontalis's interpretation has the merit of providing a contextualising framework within which to explore the nature of Sartre's involvement in politics in the postwar period. The three following chapters can therefore be read to some extent as a vindication of Pontalis's global thesis insofar as they explore different manifestations of Sartre's quest for a primary historical agent. Chapter 3, focused on Gaullism, recounts the individual intellectual's attempt to combat what is perceived as an alienating conservative ideology determined to stifle the forces of movement and change. In many ways, de Gaulle's highly idiosyncratic and individualistic politics of grandeur mirrored Sartre's own belief at a certain stage in his development in the capacity of the free individual agent to effect significant political and social change. Chapter 4, centred on the Cold War politics of the French Communist Party (PCF), explores the very real difficulties encountered by Sartre in his attempt to negotiate an acceptable settlement with a political party whose centrality to the process of historical transformation remained unquestioned for a considerable period of time. Finally, Chapter 5, dealing with the Maoist politics of a new generation of younger political activists, examines Sartre's capacity to abandon all previously held ideological positions in a process of self-renewal driven by a growing belief in the historical efficacy of the radicalism of youth. The quest for the primary historical agent, the ever-present commitment to a process of active social and political change, and the ability to re-invent an ideological position in the light of prevailing historical circumstances without residual adhesion to or nostalgia for previous positions, constitute the inner fabric of Sartre's postwar politics.

In my two previous books on Sartre, I have stressed the importance of the notions of transition and division when attempting to make sense of Sartre's intellectual and ideological itinerary. Twenty years after Sartre's death, these two interpretative schema would appear as rich and insightful as ever. To understand the specific nature of Sartre's political outlook in the postwar period it is in my view essential to examine the totality of Sartre's life span in its precise historical, social and geographical context. The aim of this introductory chapter to the first half of this book is therefore to explore the nature of Sartre's insertion within the France of 1905–80 with a view to clarifying the socio-historical structures that inscribed within Sartre's political consciousness what I perceive as a quintessentially transitional and divided political imagination. This underlying socio-historical inscription offers an explanation why Sartre appears to have inverted the trajectory of the 'conventional' political itinerary by moving from apparent political indifference as a young man to increasingly extremist and radical positions as he grew older.

HISTORICAL DIVISIONS

In any assessment of Sartre's ideological itinerary, one event unquestionably overshadows all others: the outbreak of the Second World War in 1940. The consequences of the French military defeat in 1940 were so far-reaching and profound that the totality of Sartre's existence was recast and realigned as a consequence of it. Sartre's post-1945 political and cultural development was evidently deeply influenced by wartime experience of defeat, occupation and liberation.

At the same time, however, the very significance to be attached to the period leading up to the defeat of 1940 was itself fundamentally and dramatically revised. The cosy illusions and mystifications of a politically irresponsible prewar period could no longer be sustained in the aftermath of the brutality and violence of the events of 1940–5:

> To that particular generation the breaking-point was 1940. We saw that we had been living through an absolutely faked age: since we imagined it as a rather indefinite progress towards peace we took it as such. Whatever we did seemed to us our small personal contribution to this peaceful evolution. In a way we worked with a progressive optimism with which Marxists credit the bourgeois. Meanwhile all our actions belonged to another, genuine reality, that which led to the military and civilian war of 1939. We had been fooled and we knew it. We had experienced a situation of violence, of contradictions and conflicts, a typically Marxist situation in its unfolding, just as a progressive situation flows along more or less softly and slowly. From then on, many who like myself, are in their early fifties, changed.[2]

The events of 1940–5 intruded so profoundly into Sartre's personal life-style that he was left with no choice but to re-examine the premises on which he had constructed his existence in the prewar period. It is this process of critical re-examination and scrutiny in the light of the events of 1940–5 which is the key to understanding Sartre's original contribution to the politics and culture of postwar France.

In retrospect, it is not difficult to appreciate the reasons for Sartre's depoliticised existence during the 1920s and 1930s. He was literally enmeshed within an élitist educational system that promoted and encouraged the pursuit of intellectual attainment in line with the class ideals of the French Third Republic. Born in 1905, he lived for 35 years naïvely convinced that he was somehow making a 'small personal contribution to a rather indefinite progress towards peace'.[3] His passage through the Lycée Henri IV (1915–17 and 1920–2), the Lycée at La Rochelle (1917–20), the Lycée Louis-le-Grand (1922–4) and the Ecole Normale Supérieure (1924–9), together with his years as a teacher in the Lycée Le Havre (1931–3 and 1934–6), Laon (1936–7) and the Lycée Pasteur (1937–9) are indicative of a deep immersion in the political and cultural assumptions of the Third Republic. The shattering of Republican illusions in 1940 was inevitably to lead to a fundamental reassessment of all previously held beliefs.

This interpretation of 1940 as the watershed in Sartre's existence cannot be overemphasised. After 1940 the world changed and Sartre changed with it. The comparison with Nizan is highly instructive. Not only is it worth emphasising the almost alarming differences in political awareness between Nizan and Sartre in the interwar period (and Sartre's subsequent realisation of this difference no doubt played a significant part in his increasing postwar political radicalisation); it is also appropriate to recall Nizan's assertion that '6 February 1934 marked a dividing point in literature as well as in politics'.[4] In the same way that Sartre was to experience directly the impact of history in 1940 and draw specific political and cultural conclusions from those events, so Nizan had reacted to the civil unrest in France in February 1934.

What this illustrates overall is that Sartre's postwar political itinerary cannot be disconnected from the events of

1940 and from the state of political mystification that Sartre subsequently judged himself to have been living through during the late 1920s and the 1930s. The radicalism of Sartre's postwar politics must to some degree therefore be attributed to a desire to catch up on a past political life that had somehow eluded him.

PROGRESSIVE-REGRESSIVE POLITICS

Régis Debray has accurately portrayed Sartre as a transitional political intellectual who enabled his own generation to negotiate its way more effectively towards participation in practical politics. Comparing his own generation with that of Sartre, he draws an analogy between the guilt experienced by Sartre in 1944–5 on discovering the atrocities of the existence of Nazi concentration camps, and his own sense of shame in 1960–2 arising from an awareness of the systematic use of torture in Algeria. The common denominator in both instances was a recognition of the powerlessness of the intellectual to prevent such atrocities from occurring, and the consequent need to seek atonement in political and social commitment in the present. Debray concludes:

> Sartre was the bridge to be crossed in order to reach the other bank where what he called the 'impassable philosophy of our time' awaited us ... [Sartre] acted as ferryman between the moralising attitudes of bourgeois rebellion and a more systematic participation in political projects at the centre of which was Sartre himself.[5]

In contextual terms, such a formulation places Sartre at a point of political transition between the prewar and the postwar. He bridges both periods and consequently acts inevitably as a political mediator for younger generations of French intellectuals, brokering and legitimising their passage towards more radical political solutions.

At the same time, however, he constitutes an emblematic case study of the mid-twentieth-century politicised intellectual in his own right. To use Sartre's own terminology, his political evolution is characteristically 'progressive-regressive'. Driven into a brutal recognition of the historical process in 1940, Sartre's postwar political itinerary resembles a series of pitched battles and skirmishes in which he uses intellectual tools drawn from one epoch (Third Republic France) to wage the political wars of another epoch (Fourth and Fifth Republic France). It is the growing disjunction between on the one hand Sartre's own ideological beliefs and assumptions fashioned by the experiences of a prewar period, and on the other the social and economic reality of postwar France, that constitutes the drama and the exemplarity of the case of Sartre. Expressed simply, Sartre's historical situation is such that the ideological assumptions taken on board during the Third Republic are ultimately tested in the political environment of the Fourth and Fifth Republics when, with the rapidly evolving social, economic and technological structure of an advanced capitalist state, the role of the writer/intellectual undergoes a profound change – a classic example, in other words, of 'progressive-regressive politics'.

In order to gain a sense of the global shape of this progressive-regressive political itinerary, it is appropriate in the initial stages of analysis of Sartre's political imagination to sketch out briefly the key phases in Sartre's evolution from 1945 until 1975. Unquestionably, Sartre's postwar political trajectory was determined principally by the evolving nature of his relationship with the French Communist Party, and to a lesser extent by his relationship with Gaullist and neo-Gaullist right-wing political parties that held power in France from 1958 until 1981, the year after Sartre's death: hence the decision to focus in the following three chapters on Sartre's relations with the PCF during the Cold War, on his relations with Gaullism, and on the radical 'anti-PCF' politics of Maoism in the aftermath of May 1968.

Sartre's attitude to the PCF was from the outset highly problematical. In the period following the Liberation, Sartre was inevitably viewed with suspicion by prominent communist intellectuals and party members, not merely because he had been a close friend and associate of Paul Nizan during the 1920s and 1930s (Nizan, who had resigned for the PCF in 1939 and who had been subsequently vilified by the party), but also and perhaps more importantly, because Sartre's intellectual and political activities at this time were considered to be completely detrimental to the party itself. As the charismatic leader of an existentialist philosophical/literary group that had rapidly assumed international notoriety, Sartre was accused by the communists of diverting the attention of young French men and women, the potential recruits of the PCF, away from the revolutionary ideals of Marxism towards the nihilism of existentialism. Equally, as a prominent figure in the *Rassemblement Démocratique Révolutionnaire* (RDR), a political movement founded in 1948 with the aim of 'rediscovering the great tradition of revolutionary socialism'[6] by attempting to resituate revolutionary politics between the SFIO (*Section Française de l'Internationale Ouvrière*) and the PCF, Sartre was attacked by the communists for failing to recognise that the PCF alone was the sole force capable of achieving the social transformation of France sought by the French working class. Overall the 1945–50 period witnessed Sartre attempting to deny the realities of Cold War politics, ceaselessly arguing the case both for the realignment of a radical socialist political force between the SFIO and the PCF, and for a European alternative to the divisive international solutions proposed by two antagonistic superpowers.[7]

The outbreak of the Korean War in June 1950 proved to be the catalyst that propelled Sartre closer to the PCF. At a moment when the Cold War was reaching the peak of its intensity, Sartre chose to opt for the Soviet rather than the US camp. Sartre had already been critical of American society as early as 1945.[8] In 1952 and 1954 he chose to align himself closely with the Soviet cause in a series of articles entitled 'Les Communistes et la paix'.[9] By 1954, at the height of his collaboration with Soviet communism, his glib eulogy of the Soviet state in the pro-communist newspaper, *Libération*, can only be understood as a product of Cold War propaganda.[10] The 1956 Soviet intervention in Hungary, however, brought Sartre's close relationship with the Soviet Union to an abrupt end. The publication of 'Le Fantôme de Staline' in January 1957[11] marked the beginning of what was to prove to be an ever-widening gulf between Sartre and Soviet-style communism.

Sartre's political development at this juncture was also further complicated by developments on the domestic front. The collapse of the Fourth Republic, the return to power of de Gaulle in 1958, and the continuing problems in Algeria conspired to direct Sartre's attention towards alternative forms of political activity. The 1960s witnessed a sustained effort on Sartre's part to rediscover the spirit of the revolution in numerous Third World anti-colonial struggles. From Cuba, to Algeria, to Vietnam, Sartre vociferously lent his support to indigenous populations struggling to break free from the yoke of capitalist domination. It is a curious fact that Sartre remained relatively silent on de Gaulle's presidency during the 1960s. Although Sartre had engaged in a strident polemic against de Gaulle and Gaullism in 1947[12] and throughout the Algerian crisis of the late 1950s,[13] he chose rather simply to negate the unacceptable reality of Gaullist France in the 1960s, substituting in its place the distant revolutionary scenarios of Cuba and Vietnam.

The events of May 1968 evidently transformed the political situation in France, signalling not only the imminent departure of de Gaulle, but also and more significantly, the rebirth of extremist revolutionary groups situated to the left of the Communist Party. For the first time, amid the heady atmosphere of May, an alternative revolutionary strategy seemed possible. The PCF had been outmanoeuvred by the spontaneous actions of revolutionary student groups. Sartre was no longer merely critical of the PCF. He had become openly dismissive. His public support of the students and his unequivocal condemnation of the PCF, which he castigated as the ultimate bastion of conservatism in France (*The Communists are Afraid of the Revolution*)[14] highlighted the fact that henceforth the PCF was a spent force in Sartre's eyes, and that his political allegiances would be transferred during the early to mid-1970s to the radical Maoist groups that had emerged from May. After 1968 Sartre was finally freed from the necessity to come to an accommodation with a doctrinaire Stalinist party which had never really accepted him as one of their own. Sartre was temperamentally far better suited to the more libertarian, anarchistic attitudes of the Maoist militants, with some of whom he was subsequently to form genuine friendships.

Sartre's political itinerary is consequently a tale of progressive radicalisation, a relentless journey through the complexities of revolutionary politics overshadowed for the most part by the spectre of the Cold War, a totalitarian Soviet state and a powerful French Communist Party. This notion of 'radicalism' is in fact at the very epicentre of Sartre's life and work. Assessing his own past in a highly self-critical vein in 1975, Sartre highlighted his greatest failing as his inability at certain moments in his life to act in a sufficiently radical manner:

> The point is that I have not always taken my radicalism through to its logical conclusion. I have naturally enough, for one reason or another, made many mistakes in my life, but every time that I have made a mistake, the underlying reason has been that *I have not been radical enough*. (my italics)[15]

Sartre's reservations regarding his own 'radicalism' in no way diminish the exemplary quality of his intellectual itinerary as a process of growing radicalisation. Once the primary historical lesson of 1940 had been fully understood, there was only one way forward for Sartre in the postwar period: the search for a radical intellectual and political agency that would engineer social change. This search, characterised by Pontalis as a quest for an elusive historical agent manifesting itself at different historical phases in various ideological guises, was also a search for a like-minded political community. 1940 revealed to Sartre the illusion that the individual was somehow separate from the historical process. The crushing defeat of France by German military forces rapidly exploded the myth that the destiny of the individual was disconnected from that of the broader social community.

What Sartre needed to discover in the postwar period, therefore, was not only the agency which might most effectively realise social change, but also the primary social group/community with which to work in order to achieve such change. Paradoxically, over twenty years were to pass before Sartre finally discovered both the agency and the community (youth and Maoist political groups) with which he was genuinely in sympathy and with whom he felt that he could work on terms of genuine reciprocity. The protracted and ultimately exasperating negotiations with the PCF between 1945 and 1968 were perhaps a necessary prelude in the postwar French context to the rediscovery of radicalism in the aftermath of the events of May 1968. Whatever the case, Sartre's political itinerary, a sustained and unrelenting exemplification of progressive-regressive revolutionary politics, constitutes overall both a cautionary tale in 'radicalism' and a highly significant case-study in the politics of postwar France.

3

Sartre and de Gaulle: Two Conceptions of France

1990 marked the tenth anniversary of the death of Jean-Paul Sartre[1] and the twentieth anniversary of the death and the one hundredth anniversary of the birth of Charles de Gaulle.[2] Both anniversaries were commemorated in widely publicised conferences and media events staged at the Vidéothèque de Paris: Sartre from 22–4 June, de Gaulle from 26 June until 17 July.[3] There was a curious and multiple irony in the chronological juxtaposition in this particular venue of these two conferences devoted to two highly significant figures of twentieth-century French intellectual and political history, to which I shall return later. Reference to these two commemorative media events, however, serves as a useful symbolic point of entry into a discussion of the relationship between arguably the most influential French intellectual and the most influential French political leader of the twentieth century.

My aim in this chapter is to examine the Sartre–de Gaulle relationship from three perspectives. In the first instance, I would like to make explicit the almost diametrically opposed philosophical, political and cultural assumptions that underpin their individual conceptions of France as a nation, of the role of the state, of political parties and of the electorate in French domestic politics. I shall propose that this constitutes nothing less than two irreconcilable conceptions of France and French political culture.

Second, I shall offer a critical commentary of relations between Sartre and de Gaulle in the postwar period, focusing on certain key events that took place between 1944 and 1975, events which highlight the extent to which the polemic between Sartre and de Gaulle symbolically mirrored the evolving discourses of the left and of the right from the Liberation to the Cold War to the events of May 1968 and their aftermath.

Third, and finally, I would like to propose an underlying psychological opposition between Sartre and de Gaulle based on the notions of 'rootedness' and 'rootlessness' which, in my view, provides a fundamental insight into their highly divergent political viewpoints.

FRANCE: NATION, STATE AND PEOPLE

On the first page of his war memoirs, de Gaulle articulates a strikingly clear and forthright conception of France as an integral nation state and geographically delineated homeland, and as the site of a politics of grandeur:

> Throughout my life I have always had a certain idea of France … it is an idea inspired as much by sentiment as by reason. The emotional side of my character has no difficulty in imagining France as a princess in a fairy tale or a madonna on a wall painting destined for an eminent and exceptional fate. Instinctively, I have the feeling that Providence created her for great success or exemplary misfortune. If by chance, however, her actions show any sign of mediocrity, I experience a feeling of absurdity and abnormality that is attributable to the shortcomings of the French people, not to the genius of the homeland. At the same time, the positive side of my character convinces me that France is only ever equal to herself when she is playing a leading role; that only vast projects are capable of compensating for the propensity for disintegration that its people harbours within itself; that our country ought on pain of mortal death aim high and stand tall. In brief, France cannot be France without grandeur.[4]

The principal components of de Gaulle's political vision are contained in this founding statement: the grand destiny of the French nation state, whether it be in heroic accomplishments or in exemplary failures; the differentiation between the necessary grandeur of the nation and the potential divisiveness and inadequacy of the French people; the implicit belief that de Gaulle himself would in some way be involved in such a politics of grandeur.

Allied to this belief in the special historic destiny of France was, of course, the Gaullist vision of a strong, executive-controlled state machinery that would keep in check the misguided and hence potentially dangerous activities of political parties that lacked a clear sense of national interest. De Gaulle's resolute belief in the historic role of the institutions of the state was clearly articulated in a speech that he made on a visit to Westminster Abbey and the Houses of Parliament on 7 April 1960. Alluding to what he judged to be the exceptional fortitude of Britain during the darkest hours of the Second World War, he remarked:

> Your deep-rooted national qualities enabled you to play an exceptional role at the height of the storm; how very important also, however, were your invaluable institutions! In the darkest hour, who even thought of calling into question the legitimacy and the authority of the State?[5]

De Gaulle here characteristically explains the resilience of Britain during the Second World War as a function of a national specificity based on the established institutions of the state. The allusion to the early days of the war is not innocent. There is a recurrent mythical reference system in de Gaulle's imagination which links political and social activity with a particular moment of historical adversity which was overcome through the fortitude and strength of character of particular individuals and through the historical solidity and ultimate justice of state institutions. Encoded in this entire discourse is the Gaullist belief in strong executive leadership and in disciplined and tightly controlled state institutional structures, and an implicit rejection of lax party political ambitions or popular grass-roots activism that escape from executive control.

Sartre's approach to nation, state and people was of course very different. Whereas de Gaulle was essentially preoccupied with national and state institutional structures which embodied the national will, and which enabled men and women of stature to meet the challenges of adverse situations, and also prevented the weak-willed majority from disgracing the nation, Sartre's central concerns were the democratic rights of ordinary men and women, and their capacity to act within the framework of alienating state structures.

Although, for quite different reasons, Sartre and de Gaulle shared a healthy scepticism towards traditional party politics, there was little other common ground between them. Ultimately, Sartre rejected all forms of state institutional control and regulation as oppressive and alienating, preferring instead what he considered to be the authentic aims and aspirations of the mass of the people struggling for liberation from the state and its stultifying institutional structures. To take a striking example, Sartre perceived a fundamental distinction between the justice of the state, to which de Gaulle pays homage, and what he refers to as 'primitive justice' which stands outside state control:

> In France there are two kinds of justice. One is bureaucratic justice, which ties the proletariat to its condition. The other is primitive justice, which is the profound movement of the proletariat and the common people asserting their freedom against proletariatization. When de Gaulle declares that all Justice belongs to the State, he is either mistaken or showing his true character, for the source of all justice is the people. The government takes advantage of the tendency towards justice that it finds in the common people and creates organs of justice that represent the bureaucratization of the people's will to justice. These

> courts pass judgement by simply applying the law, and they draw their inspiration from bourgeois principles. Thus they are based on fraud and a falsification of the popular will. In choosing between the two kinds of justice, the one codified and permanent, the other irregular and primitive, you must therefore be aware that they are contradictory. If you choose one, you will be held accountable by the other ... I have chosen popular justice as the deeper form of justice, the only true justice.[6]

The profound differences in thinking between Sartre and de Gaulle could hardly be expressed more graphically. Whereas de Gaulle elevates the state and its institutions to a privileged position in his political and ethical value system, and interprets the actions of the people as misguided deviations and errors that must be held in check by executive control, Sartre elevates to an almost mystical level the daily struggle of the people against what he designates as the 'serialising' propensity of state institutions. Authentic political values are not located in the regal institutions of the state, but rather in the constant battle of the people to defend themselves against absorption within the state machinery.

Another primary example of a state institution which elicits polarised responses from Sartre and de Gaulle is the voting system. De Gaulle not only finds personal and political legitimisation in the process of democratic election, but also perceives in it the founding principle of the presidential system of the Fifth Republic. Sartre, on the other hand, rejects the voting system as yet another technique of state manipulation and mystification:

> When I vote, I abdicate my power – that is, the possibility everyone has of joining others to form a sovereign group, which would have no need of representatives. By voting I confirm the fact that we, the voters, are always other than ourselves and that none of us can ever desert seriality in favour of the group, except through intermediaries.

> For the serialised citizen, to vote is undoubtedly to give his support to a party. But it is even more to vote for voting … that is, to vote for the political institution that keeps us in a state of powerless serialisation.
>
> We saw this in 1968 when de Gaulle asked the people of France, who had risen and formed groups, to vote – in other words, to lie down again and retreat into seriality. The non-institutional groups fell apart and the voters, identical and separate, voted for the UDR. The party promised to defend them against the action of groups which they themselves had belonged to a few days earlier … The voter must remain lying down, steeped in his own powerlessness. He will thus choose parties so that they can exert *their* authority and not his. Each man … will choose his masters for the next four years without seeing that this so-called right to vote is simply the refusal to allow him to unite with others in resolving the true problems by *praxis*.[7]

Quite clearly, Sartre and de Gaulle, operating at opposite ends of the political and cultural spectrum, symbolised two radically different visions of France and French political culture. The manner in which such deep-rooted differences manifested themselves in practical politics in the postwar period is the subject of the next part of my analysis.

SARTRE, DE GAULLE AND GAULLISM: 1944–75

An account of relations between Sartre, de Gaulle and Gaullism from 1944 until 1975 offers an illuminating picture of the ideological, political and cultural landscape of postwar France. Although Sartre and de Gaulle inhabited entirely different social environments, and although their encounters were essentially conducted at a distance as a part of an ongoing public debate, they nonetheless gradually assumed a leadership function symbolising alternative visions of social, political and cultural development: left versus right, libertarianism versus authoritarianism, internationalism versus nationalism, and so on. So that in many ways they each became a symbol of a particular world view to which different social groups maintained allegiance. What I would like to offer here in the first instance is a panoramic overview of the key moments in the development of their public encounters, focusing principally on Sartre's perception of and reaction to de Gaulle, and then subsequently I shall assess critically the significance of this interconnected public itinerary.

Paradoxically, the initial encounter between the two was far from antagonistic. Sartre's account of the liberation of Paris in a series of articles for *Combat* written in 1944 is a case in point. It is quite noticeable that when Sartre evoked the victorious march-past in the capital during which shots were fired in the direction of General de Gaulle, he bore no particular animosity to the general, who was simply presented as the natural leader of the French nation.[8] Equally, and more significantly, the first of the series of articles that Sartre wrote for *Le Figaro* during a subsequent trip to the United States from January until July 1945 constituted nothing less than an explicit defence of de Gaulle and Gaullism, an attempt to defend de Gaulle against American prejudice.

The American distrust of de Gaulle during the war is in fact well documented by de Gaulle himself.[9] Considered as a potential ally of communism, de Gaulle was marginalised in favour of Giraud, whom the Americans attempted to promote as the leader of the Free French. Sartre undoubtedly perceived the American decision to invite a group of pro-resistance journalists to visit the USA as an attempt to smooth over the troubled waters of Franco-British/American relations since 1940. Typically, Sartre was unwilling to be politely accommodating and insisted on clarifying matters in his own inimitable style:

> The Americans [declared Sartre] were inclined to judge the French on the home front from those who had emigrated

> and it has been said that these were in their majority supporters of Pétain ... I do not want to give names. But I must say that certain French journalists ... bought by high finance or subsidised by the State Department, published a newspaper that did great harm to our cause.[10]

This latter comment, in particular, provoked an acrimonious dispute centred not only on the patriotism of French citizens who had taken refuge in the USA after 1940, but also on the role of the American government in promoting a certain image of France.[11] Sartre's aim was doubtless to clear the air, to signify to both his French and American readerships that a new, post-liberation era had dawned in France, and that the Vichy image of France as 'fearful' and 'withdrawn' was to be replaced by a Gaullist image of France as 'revolutionary'. 'If Gaullism has triumphed in America', Sartre concluded in a paradoxically Gaullist tone:

> it has not done so in its status as a party or a sectarian group. The victory of de Gaulle in what has sometimes been called the battle of New York signifies the victory of one image of France over another.[12]

Sartre's underlying opposition to de Gaulle and Gaullism was evidently masked in 1945 by the image of de Gaulle as resistance leader and opponent of Pétain and Giraud.

This honeymoon period in their relations was not to last long, however. Two years after Sartre's visit to the USA, the postwar political polarisation between left and right, between pro-communist and pro-capitalist camps, was well under way. De Gaulle had become the undisputed political leader of the increasingly powerful right-wing Rassemblement du Peuple Français (RPF), and Sartre had assumed the intellectual leadership of the increasingly influential review *Les Temps Modernes*. The first moment of political confrontation in fact originated in the series of radio programmes broadcast by the *Temps Modernes* group in October 1947. The very first of these radio broadcasts was entitled 'Le Gaullisme et le RPF' ('Gaullism and the RPF').[13]

The extent to which relations between Sartre and de Gaulle had degenerated between 1945 and 1947 can be demonstrated by reference to the polemical dispute that was sparked off by a comparison made by Bonafé, one of the members of the *Temps Modernes* group, between General de Gaulle as portrayed in an RPF political poster and Adolf Hitler. This particularly acrimonious incident was significant in a number of ways and with hindsight can be seen to have established the fundamentally antagonistic tenor of Sartre's relations with de Gaulle and Gaullism from that moment on.

In the aftermath of the first broadcast, when the de Gaulle/Hitler comparison was alluded to, Henry Torres and General Guillain de Bénouville, both well-known Gaullists, were sufficiently incensed not merely to refuse to participate in a debate with Sartre on the RPF as they had initially agreed, but also, according to Sartre himself, proceeded to abuse him verbally in the crudest of terms. This incident consequently not only led to antagonistic relations between Sartre and Gaullism, but also marked the beginning of the estranged relationship between Sartre and Raymond Aron. In Sartre's eyes, Aron, who had been called upon to act as mediator in the dispute, merely lent his support to the two Gaullists. In many ways, Sartre's notorious and highly personalised attack on Aron in the aftermath of the events of May 1968 ('Les Bastilles de Raymond Aron')[14] constitutes an act of retribution for this perceived lack of support in 1947 when Aron was drawing ever closer to Gaullism.

At a substantive level, the attack on de Gaulle and Gaullism in these broadcasts is located at three levels. Leaving aside the personal abuse already mentioned (Bonafé), there is a rejection of de Gaulle's cult of the individual capable of rising above the masses to assume power at moments of crisis (Pontalis); fears are expressed at de Gaulle's hidden social and political agenda; the absence, for example, of any clearly defined socio-economic programme is considered to be highly suspicious (Beauvoir);

and de Gaulle's allegedly provocative militarism is condemned, a militarism based alternately on association with the United States against the USSR or on association with other European states against both blocs (Sartre and Merleau-Ponty).

With the gradual demise of the RPF during the late 1940s and early 1950s, a consequence of de Gaulle's withdrawal from what he considered to be the small-minded and divisive party politics of the Fourth Republic, interaction between Sartre and de Gaulle was fairly limited. De Gaulle went into self-imposed exile awaiting grander political events, Sartre spent a decade negotiating a fellow travelling position in relation to the French communist party. The crisis in Algeria and the subsequent return to power of de Gaulle in 1958, however, were to bring deep-rooted antagonisms between them to the surface. This was particularly the case as far as Sartre was concerned, who judged de Gaulle's return to power to be no less than a major calamity for France.

The events of 1958 consequently enabled Sartre to develop further his opposition to what he perceived as de Gaulle's paternalistic, dictatorial attitude to the French people. Whereas in 1947 there was a tendency to refute de Gaulle's ideas by portraying him somewhat abusively as the mouthpiece of an incipient fascism, in 1958 emphasis was given at one level to highlighting de Gaulle's distant, patriarchical style of leadership, and at another to disclosing the underlying economic, social and political factors which made recourse to de Gaulle necessary.

In a series of articles published in *L'Express*,[15] Sartre offered a highly critical account of de Gaulle's accession to power and of the setting up of the Fifth Republic. With the gradual collapse of ministerial authority and of the moral integrity of the governments of the Fourth Republic under the pressure of events in Algeria, de Gaulle, the leader of the Free French during the war, was perceived by the majority of the French nation as the only remaining political solution to the crisis. Sartre refused to accept, however, either that there was no alternative to a Gaullist '*coup d'état*', or that de Gaulle himself would not recoil from installing a dictatorship:

> When [de Gaulle] stated in all honesty that he would not take it into his head at the age of sixty-seven to impose a dictatorship he was left with a simple alternative: give up power ... or become a dictator. For the situation decides.[16]

Sartre was particularly dismissive of the charismatic aura of de Gaulle, of his isolated and distant attitude to the French people, of his continuing silence regarding his underlying political intentions, a silence that Sartre interpreted as a form of psychological blackmail on the electorate:

> the solitude of this man enclosed within his grandeur prevents him, whatever the circumstances, from becoming the leader of a Republican state. Or, what comes down to the same thing, prevents the state of which he will be the leader from remaining a Republic.[17]

Sartre's comments on the Fifth Republic constitution echo his comments on de Gaulle as the imminent dictator. They represent a refusal to acknowledge either the legality or the desirability of an executive-based constitutional framework. Not only, Sartre maintained, would de Gaulle's elective monarchy fundamentally weaken the natural sovereignty of the people in the French Republican system, but also the process whereby such a system was being brought into being was itself illegal: 'We are told that we are going to vote: this is a lie. Let us tear away the tissue of words that covers a crime: 28 September will not be a day of election, but a day of violence'.[18]

Although centred principally on the persona of de Gaulle and on the intrinsically anti-democratic nature of the proposed constitution. Sartre's analysis also ranged over broader economic, social and political issues. At one level, he attempted to understand the psychological state of the majority of the French nation whom, he concluded, would almost certainly vote 'Yes' in the referendum, and thereby support de Gaulle. His diagnosis was that the French electorate was gripped by fear and by a sense of powerlessness originating in the relatively insignificant status of France on the stage of international diplomacy, and in the directionless and incoherent domestic policies pursued by successive governments under the Fourth Republic.

At another level, Sartre was insistent that the problems of France in 1958 could not be resolved through a sterile discussion of the relative merits of executive and legislative constitutional powers, but must be envisaged in a wider socio-economic framework: the introduction of the Marshall Plan and the onset of the Cold War, the progressive bankruptcy of political legitimacy under the Fourth Republic, the gradual disintegration of the forces of the democratic left, and, in particular, the increasingly problematical status of the French military which, following the catastrophic defeat of 1940, simply lost its way on distant colonial battlefields, initially in Indochina, subsequently in Algeria. 'The army is protecting its own interests in Algeria. Without [Algeria] what would it be?', he asked rhetorically; 'Departure from Algeria would mean the death of our army.'[19] In Sartre's eyes, the recourse to de Gaulle in 1958 was above all the product of the failure on the part of the French to redefine the role of their military forces in a nuclear age, and especially to take cognisance of what he refers to as 'the most significant event of the second half of this century: the birth of nationalism among the peoples of Africa and Asia'.[20]

This final parting shot against de Gaulle in which Sartre invoked the spectre of 'third worldism' was in fact highly significant. 1958 was of course a major victory for de Gaulle and nothing short of a catastrophe for Sartre. The establishment of de Gaulle's Presidential Republican system was not simply an anathema to Sartre personally. It represented in his eyes the humiliation and defeat of the entire French left. It was as if the French nation had submitted to the will of an authoritarian father figure. It is worth noting in this respect that at this very moment Sartre was working not only on a preliminary draft of his autobiography,[21] but also on a film script of a life of Freud,[22] in both of which the central issue of dominant father figures was doubtless analysed and represented through the increasingly powerful and authoritarian presence of President de Gaulle.[23]

Sartre's only recourse in this highly dispiriting situation was to direct his political energies to the third world revolutionary struggles of Algeria, Cuba and Vietnam, where the unpalatable political realities of an ascendant right-wing Gaullist regime could be symbolically denied. For the next ten years, therefore, Sartre committed himself to political causes in the Third World and averted his gaze from French domestic politics. In 1967, however, at the height of de Gaulle's power, there was none the less an intriguing exchange of views between the two of them, motivated by the escalating conflict in Vietnam.

During the summer of 1966 Lord Bertrand Russell had invited Sartre to participate in an 'International Tribunal Against War Crimes in Vietnam'. Following the inaugural meeting of the Russell Tribunal held in London on 14 and 15 November 1966, Sartre was quick to publicise the intentions of the group. Their aim, he maintained, was not simply to condemn American atrocities in Vietnam from a moral perspective, but rather to determine whether or not American actions in Vietnam constituted a breach of the international legislation on war crimes as established at the Nuremberg trials. The objective, in short, was to judge American imperialism by its own laws.[24]

In April 1967 Sartre wrote to de Gaulle requesting that Vladimir Dedijer, the then president of the Russell Tribunal, be granted a visa allowing him to stay in France to chair the sessions of the tribunal scheduled to take place in Paris. De Gaulle's public refusal to grant Dedijer a visa, thereby preventing the group from meeting in Paris, not merely provided Sartre with the opportunity to publicise once again the activities of the Russell Tribunal itself, but also constituted yet another twist in the saga of relations between Sartre and de Gaulle in the postwar period.

The correspondence between Sartre and de Gaulle on this matter is illuminating.[25] Sartre dismisses de Gaulle's claim that the latter sympathises with the political viewpoint of the Russell Tribunal, but that he nonetheless feels a sense of obligation to the United States, a political ally in the sphere of international diplomacy. Sartre interprets de Gaulle's response as no more than political expediency in both the domestic and foreign policy spheres: in Sartre's eyes, the Americans had simply threatened de Gaulle with economic sanctions were he to resist their Vietnam policy; equally, recent electoral setbacks on the domestic front had encouraged the Gaullists to seek support from 'Atlanticist' liberals such as Lecanuet and Giscard d'Estaing.[26]

More significant as far as the Sartre–de Gaulle relationship is concerned, however, is Sartre's interpretation of the political significance of de Gaulle's actions in this particular incident:

> For de Gaulle, the government should not depend on the country but should keep itself above it, without ever allowing it to participate directly in its actions. A country, however, is not limited to its government. The attitude which consists in mildly rebuking the policy of the United States whilst preventing the mass of the people from demonstrating their opposition to the war in Vietnam is totally undemocratic … This approach is typically Gaullist: the leader has his ideas on Vietnam, he sometimes expresses these ideas in speeches – adding at the same time that he is unable for the moment to do anything effective whatsoever – but above all he does not want his viewpoint to be popularised, supported by the masses, because that would link him to them, and that is deep down what he detests most …

> The Gaullist conception of justice ... leads to the complete submission of the magistrature to the State. True justice ought to draw its strength both from the State and from the mass of the people. This is how justice was conceived during the French revolution: the jury was set up in order to enable the citizen to participate in justice.[27]

These fundamental differences between Sartre and de Gaulle regarding the nature of the relationship between government élites and the people, and of the nature of popular justice, were to come to a head in the events of May 1968. By the late 1960s, Sartre had decided to abandon all pretence at moderating his tone when speaking of de Gaulle:

> I reproach myself personally for having been far too respectful towards de Gaulle in my articles. I should not have taken into account the fact that he was respected by a large number of French people, thereby signalling respect for this respect. I should have attacked him directly as a dangerous individual.[28]

The events of May 1968 provided Sartre with precisely the context that he had been waiting for to deliver a broadside attack on de Gaulle and Gaullism.

Four key interviews were published in *Le Nouvel observateur* between May and November 1968 in which Sartre unequivocally condemned both Gaullism and Raymond Aron, symbols of an outmoded political regime and an outmoded educational system.[29] In the first interview, given at the height of the events on 20 May 1968, Sartre was content to play a relatively subdued role, granting maximum visibility to the student leader, Daniel Cohn-Bendit. In subsequent interviews, however, given in June, July and November, when the political advantage had been regained by the right, Sartre was much more forthright and combative. In June he launched a blistering personal attack on Raymond Aron, alleging that Aron was unworthy of his status and position in the university sector because he had never called his ideas into question, had never submitted his ideas to the test of student opinion: 'Now that the whole of France has seen de Gaulle naked', noted Sartre, 'the students must be able to have a look at Aron naked'.[30] Sartre's amalgamation of de Gaulle and Aron was not innocent. This was Sartre's ultimate moment of public retribution towards Aron for the 1947 Torres–Bénouville incident in which Aron had been judged to have given his support to de Gaulle and Gaullism rather than to Sartre's *Temps Modernes* group.

In June–July, following the virtual cessation of strike activities and the return to order symbolised by the first round of the legislative elections, Sartre countered the proposition that May 68 had ultimately been a failure, arguing that it was important to explore all means by which the lessons of 1968 could be profitably developed in the future.

Finally, in November 1968 Sartre delivered a vitriolic attack against Gaullism, a regime symbolising in his eyes naked class oppression:

> The armed and bloody repression, the maintenance of the existing disorder by the uniformed bunch that is called the forces of order, is merely a specific example of the repressive action that is constantly being carried out against the workers in the society in which we live.[31]

This sudden and quire dramatic change of emphasis in which the discourse of the heady atmosphere of May was replaced by the discourse of overt class warfare, coincided with a government crackdown in the sphere of law and order, and a simultaneous hardening of attitudes on the part of revolutionary activists. From this moment on, Sartre gravitated under the force of circumstances ever closer to the revolutionary left, and ever further not merely from the authoritarian and reactionary stance of de Gaulle and Gaullism, but more significantly perhaps from the traditional political class, from conventional party politics, from the established structure of the regime itself.

The events of May 1968 came as a surprise to both Sartre and de Gaulle. Sartre subsequently conceded that he had not fully understood the significance and the impact of May 68 until over one year later.[32] Whereas for Sartre, however, May 68 was a source of fundamental reappraisal and ultimately of rejuvenation, for de Gaulle the opposite was the case. May 68 had not only come as a terrible shock to de Gaulle. It had also revealed the extent to which de Gaulle was completely out of touch with the mood of the times. Although the elections of June 68 re-established an overwhelming parliamentary majority for the right, the credibility of de Gaulle as president had been fundamentally undermined. His departure from office in April 1969 in the aftermath of the referendum on the reform of the Senate and of regional councils can in many ways be interpreted as an act of political suicide by an ageing statesman aware that his time was up. In contrast, Sartre underwent a progressive radicalisation in his political outlook, developing his links both with extreme left-wing Maoist groups and with revolutionary publications such as *La Cause du Peuple*.

The ten years spanning 1958 and 1968 therefore constitute a pivotal moment in the Sartre–de Gaulle relationship. 1958 was a moment of crowning achievement for de Gaulle, not only personally, but also in terms of institutional reform. For Sartre 1958 was, in contrast, a moment of deep despair in which everything that he cherished appeared to be torn asunder. The entire democratic, republican infrastructure of France had in Sartre's eyes been subverted by what he considered to be the arrogant ambitions of an authoritarian leader who had seized power through the strategic manipulation of a crisis. 1968, in contrast, saw the rebirth of the forces of the libertarian left and the beginning of the end for de Gaulle's term of office.

The debate on the relative significance of May 1958 and May 1968 continues to this day. The Fifth Republican regime, the presidential system, remains in place despite periods of political cohabitation during the 1980s and 1990s. Its resilience to changing political circumstances cannot be denied. And yet, the fundamental change in outlook brought about by the events of May 1968 cannot be ignored either. After 1968 the cultural, ideological and political climate in France could never be the same again. In many ways, therefore, 1958 and 1968 symbolically represent the differing contributions to French political culture of de Gaulle and Sartre.

De Gaulle's departure from office in April 1969 was followed by his death in November 1970. The final twist in the Sartre–de Gaulle relationship, however, did not end with the general's death. Four years later, just after the accession to power of Valéry Giscard d'Estaing, Sartre was given the opportunity to make a series of television programmes, one sign among many of the new president's liberalising tendencies. The events surrounding this television history series marked the final chapter in the Sartre–de Gaulle saga.

I have analysed this particular event in some detail elsewhere.[33] What I would like to highlight in this context is the manner in which it adds a further dimension to the relationship between Sartre and de Gaulle/Gaullism. When assessing this envisaged television history series, it is important not to lose sight of the socio-political context of the time. Following Giscard d'Estaing's election as president in May 1974, radical reform of the audiovisual sphere seemed to be on the political agenda. The break-up of the ORTF (*Organisation de la Radio-Télévision Française*) was imminent, and the new managing director of the second channel, M. Marcel Jullian, appeared especially keen to develop a more radical approach to broadcasting.

On 19 November 1974, there appeared a highly provocative interview in *Libération*, the tone of which was sufficiently combative to forewarn the conservative government in power that a media coup was being orchestrated against the forces of the establishment. The reaction of the establishment was swift and decisive. Jacques Chirac, the then prime minister, immediately contacted Marcel Jullian by telephone in order to underline his opposition to the television series. Jean-Didier Wolfromm, Jullian's personal assistant at the time, who witnessed this telephone conversation, recalls the words of the prime minister as follows:

> I have a great admiration for Sartre as a philosopher, but I cannot, and will not authorise him to speak on French television in order to destroy a society which he has always hated.[34]

It is consequently clear that throughout this affair, at a moment when a liberalising Giscardianism appeared to be in the ascendancy, there was none the less in the wings a deeply ingrained Gaullist suspicion of this attempt to liberate the audiovisual sphere, a suspicion that had a long pedigree, and that in Sartre's case went back to the antagonisms engendered by the 1947 *Temps Modernes* radio series. After a lengthy series of skirmishes between Sartre, the television authorities and the Gaullist/Giscardian government of the day, Sartre withdrew from the project on 23 September 1975, alleging that his freedom of expression was being seriously compromised.

Ultimately, there can be little doubt that the eventual failure to produce this television series was the result of government censorship. Both Maurice Clavel and Jean-Didier Wolfromm were convinced of it.[35] When Robert-André Vivien, Gaullist deputy, president of the commission monitoring the financial management of the ORTF in 1974–5, and member of the board of directors of Antenne 2, subsequently described Sartre's television series in the following terms: 'ten programmes ... in which Jews, war veterans, freemasons, everybody was taken to task',[36] he demonstrated not only his political prejudices, but also the motive underlying his decision to censor the series. A Gaullist prime minister (Jacques Chirac) and a Gaullist deputy (Robert-André Vivien), both committed to a Gaullist vision of television as the 'Voice of France', could not countenance in 1975 that left-wing intellectuals such as Sartre be allowed to broadcast on a state television channel an image of society that they did not accept.

It is in this sense that the 1974–5 television history series constituted the last episode in relations between Sartre and de Gaulle. The single most significant aspect of the thirty-page synopsis of this television series is in fact the absence of de Gaulle and Gaullism. It is an absence which speaks volumes. The political activity of de Gaulle between 1962 and 1969 is simply not mentioned. 'Nothing of great importance occurred between 1962 and 1968', notes Sartre.[37] This elimination of de Gaulle from the historical process is, of course, highly significant.

The Gaullist hostility directed at the television series by Jacques Chirac and Robert-André Vivien has already been emphasised. It would appear, for example, that they were particularly opposed to the participation of Daniel Cohn-Bendit in the programme centred on May 68.[38] In many ways their hostility is hardly surprising. In November 1974 Sartre had publicly announced: 'I detested de Gaulle as much as I had detested Pétain under Vichy'.[39] Moreover, Sartre's political activities in 1974–5 were unlikely to have reassured the Gaullists in power. On 2 December 1974, for example, Sartre, Gavi and Victor called a press conference to publicise their book, *On a raison de se révolter*, a highly critical assessment of the conservative establishment, the royalties of which were to be used to finance *Libération*, a new radical, populist newspaper. On 4 December, in the company of Pierre Victor, Klaus Croissant and Daniel Cohn-Bendit, Sartre visited Andreas Baader in Stammhein prison in Stuttgart in order to draw attention to the conditions in which political prisoners were held. Political activity of this kind could only have made Gaullists more determined to prevent Sartre from exploiting state television to broadcast his subversive ideas.

To be aware of the polemical dispute surrounding this controversial television history series is to be aware of the existence of two radically opposed conceptions of society, one Gaullist, the other Sartrean, the supporters of both camps refusing any concession to the other. Sartre's television history series would have been a 'counter-history' of contemporary France, a Sartrean vision of France at the other extreme to a Gaullist vision. It would have constituted an alternative to the television series entitled '*Ces années-là*' ('Those Years') broadcast on Channel 1 in 1975, and presented by Michel Droit, 'a friend of the government'.[40] It would have been an exemplary illustration of the manner in which Sartre represented the France of the powerless, of the underprivileged and of the dispossessed.

ROOTEDNESS AND ROOTLESSNESS

It is instructive to speculate at this juncture on the overall significance of these highly divergent conceptions of the nation, state and people of France as articulated by de Gaulle and Sartre. It goes without saying that these two visions necessarily became symbolic points of reference in the evolution of French political culture in the postwar period. France's traditional political 'exceptionalism', its intrinsic affinity with conflictual rather than with consensual modes of ordering its social development, found in the polarised libertarian and authoritarian discourses of Sartre and de Gaulle a perfect sounding board for the left–right dichotomy that dominated the political landscape after 1945.

Underlying these two political visions are quite distinct psychological and cultural premises. De Gaulle's world view, however grandiose and grandiloquent it might appear, is none the less firmly and intractably rooted in a nationally defined geographical space and cultural heritage. The essence of de Gaulle's vision, in short, is a clear sense of belonging to a national community, a rootedness in a cultural area specified as France. Sartre's vision, on the other hand, is quite different. It originates in a sense of alienation, of separation and of difference. At its most prosaic level, this translates as an uneasy distancing from his class origins, but it goes way beyond this and permeates to the very core of Sartre's physical, metaphysical, philosophical, and political being.

It seems to me that this fundamental attitude of estrangement in Sartre's personality has most accurately been described by Benny Lévy as follows: 'It is to the extent that Sartre was in exile, to the extent that he was an outsider to the world, yet to the extent he inhabited the French language, that he was French'.[11] Despite his intimate involvement with the French language, Sartre none the less retained an outsider's view of France. His lack of allegiance to any particular community, or at the very least his unwillingness to be entrapped within privileged communities, and his consequent ability to empathise with all those less fortunate, dispossessed and exploited members of society, explain his own idiosyncratically anti-authoritarian vision of French political culture. The defining quality of Sartre's vision, in other words, was his rootlessness. It should come as no surprise that the original title of his autobiography was *Jean sans terre* (*Rootless John*).

The multiple irony of the juxtaposition of the two conferences held in the Vidéothèque de Paris in 1990, and to which I referred at the outset, should now be apparent. Even ten years after the death of Sartre, and almost twenty years after the death of de Gaulle, the competition between the two of them continued. Two media events organised in a venue ultimately falling under the jurisdiction of the Gaullist Mayor of Paris, Jacques Chirac, inevitably stood in ironic counterpoint one to another, a symbolic interrogation of the validity of two seemingly irreconcilable conceptions of France.

Given the greater public visibility of the de Gaulle centenary celebrations, it might have appeared that the final historical verdict had come down on the side of 'grandeur', state institutions and executive leadership. However, such an interpretation may be premature. Although it is notoriously difficult to assess the precise nature of individual contributions to a given nation's political and cultural legacy, it would appear at one level that both Gaullist and Sartrean visions have been overtaken by the events of the late 1980s and the 1990s: the Gaullist ideal of the strong and relatively autonomous nation state has been superseded by a European vision that privileges federal structures and transnational co-operation; equally, Sartre's libertarian, anti-statist politics have been undermined by the collapse of left-wing ideology and transformations brought about by the media society.

And yet, at another level, the underlying ethical and cultural impulses of both remain: the Gaullist belief in a clear sense of personal identity based principally on an allegiance to a defined geographical space, what I referred to as de Gaulle's rootedness; the Sartrean commitment to liberation from alienating social restrictions and oppression through individual and social praxis, what I have designated as Sartre's rootlessness. Perhaps, after all, the media celebrations held at the Vidéothèque de Paris twenty years ago were less ironic, more exemplary in outlook, a symbolic display of those aspects of intellectual and political leadership, both Sartrean and Gaullist, that might usefully be of service to citizens in the twenty-first century.

4

Sartre and the Nizan Affair: The Cold War Politics of French Communism

It is both fascinating and chastening to speculate on the manner in which the Sartre–Nizan relationship might have developed had Nizan survived the war, and had he experienced the socio-political realities of post-Liberation France. In many ways this process of speculation and fictional reconstruction has the makings of a promising novel, but a novel veering either towards the romantic or the pessimistic depending on one's view of the two individuals concerned and of the intellectual climate of the time.

In Michel Contat's eyes, for example, Nizan could have become the leading figure in a viable, non-communist, left-wing political group, effectively challenging the supremacy of a Stalinist-dominated French communist party.[1] As such, he would have prevented Sartre's eventual embrace of the PCF between 1950 and 1956, an embrace explicable in Contat's opinion as a product of Sartre's naïve, abstract, outsider's view of the party machine, bureaucracy and *modus vivendi*. Nizan's intimate, insider's view of the realities of the party, in contrast, would have provided Sartre with credible political leadership in a similar fashion to that given by Merleau-Ponty during the late 1940s and early 1950s. Contat does not propose any form of conclusion to this fictional reconstruction, merely the general lines of an argument that Nizan's political presence and political experience would have offered Sartre a concrete alternative model, that itself would have been the basis of a continuing postwar friendship.

This somewhat romanticised version of the Sartre–Nizan relationship is unequivocally contested by Liliane Siegel, the fifth woman in Sartre's life, author of *La Clandestine*.[2] Sartre's idealised vision as set out in the preface to *Aden Arabie*, she maintains, is explained above all precisely by the fact that Nizan died in 1940, and therefore in the post war period did not in any sense of the word constitute an intellectual rival to Sartre, unlike Aron, Camus and Merleau-Ponty, for example. In her opinion, during the 1930s Sartre and Nizan were not competing with one another intellectually. Although both had great literary ambitions, Sartre's primary concerns were philosophical, whereas Nizan's were political. In the postwar period, however, given Sartre's growing interest in politics, given his spectacular rise to fame and celebrity status, given what he himself has described as his 'imperialistic' attitude to interpersonal relationships,[3] ultimately even Nizan would have been perceived as a rival. In the end, he would have been excommunicated from the Sartre inner circle like so many others.[4] This particular version of the Sartre–Nizan myth outlined by Liliane Siegel is manifestly pessimistic and stands in marked contrast to Contat's and Sartre's own retrospective endorsement of the unique standing of Nizan in Sartre's life.

These two divergent fictional reconstructions are based on different sets of premises, the first political, the second personal and intellectual. In the first version, political strategy constitutes the basis of continuing friendship; in the second, personal and intellectual rivalry is at the root of individual animosity. Whichever version of events is the more plausible, however, what is clear is not only that in the postwar period both Sartre and Nizan would have been truly political intellectuals, but also that the personal and the political would have been inextricably intermeshed. It is this intermeshing that constitutes the real interest of the Nizan Affair of 1947, since on the one hand it provides an insight into the nature of the relationship between two prominent and representative left-wing intellectuals, and on the other it offers a snapshot of the developing post-Liberation intellectual climate at the precise moment of transition into the Cold War.

I have divided my comments into four parts. I would like initially to examine certain temperamental affinities between Sartre and Nizan with specific reference to Marxism and communism. Subsequently, I aim to assess the relationship of both Sartre and Nizan to the French Communist Party (PCF). Here, it is essential to locate the origins of the Nizan Affair in Nizan's resignation from the party in 1939, and to examine the party's general attitude to Sartre in the 1945–50 period. Finally, I shall focus specifically on the Nizan Affair of 1947.

SARTRE–NIZAN: TEMPERAMENTAL AFFINITIES AND IDEOLOGICAL CONTRADICTIONS

In 1974 Sartre declared to Simone de Beauvoir that throughout his life his only true friendships had been with a number of women (including, of course, the pivotal relationship with Simone de Beauvoir herself) and with Paul Nizan. Nizan is singled out as the primary male relationship in his life.[5] A year later, in the celebrated interview with Michel Contat on his seventieth birthday,[6] Sartre makes it clear that despite an underlying intellectual and emotional affinity between Nizan and himself that developed during the 1920s, despite the fact that Nizan was the only one of his peers to have influenced him intellectually, albeit marginally, an ideological rift nonetheless came between them during the 1930s in the shape of Marxism. Nizan's membership of the PCF and his consequent allegiance to Marxist ideology created tensions, dissonances in their relationship:

> What kept us apart from each other was that he became a Marxist, that is to say, when we became friends he

> adopted a set of ideas that was not yet his own and which had far more profound implications than he could have imagined. Consequently I was faced with a set of ideas that I barely understood ... and this set of ideas became a damned nuisance, an unpleasant practical joke because someone whom I liked was using it both as a fundamental truth and as a hoax that he was playing on me.
>
> *I felt threatened by Marxism because it represented the ideas of a friend and these ideas were cutting across our friendship.* (my italics)[7]

It is not an overstatement, moreover, to maintain that the entire history of the Sartre–Nizan relationship is the history of personal affinities complicated by political and ideological beliefs. The publication in 1990 of a thinly disguised autobiographical novel, 'La Semence et Le Scaphandre',[8] clarifies the extent of Sartre's personal affinity with Nizan. What emerges from this text written by Sartre in 1924 is the image of a juvenile relationship in which the dominant partner is unquestionably Nizan. Sartre (Tailleur) emerges as fascinated by and emotionally dependent on Nizan (Lucelles). This original personal affinity was subsequently overshadowed by the advent of communism in Nizan's life during the 1930s, and only began to reassert itself after Nizan's resignation from the PCF in 1939 and his death in 1940.

Sartre's writings of the early-to-middle 1940s are saturated with allusions to Nizan. It is significant, for example, as Geneviève Idt has demonstrated,[9] that *Les Chemins de la liberté* appears to change direction during the second part of *La Mort dans l'âme* in order to foreground the Brunet–Schneider/Vicarios confrontation linked to the policy reversal of the Nazi–Soviet pact and with clear references to Nizan's resignation from the party. The depth of feeling present in Sartre's account of the Schneider–Vicarios incident in 'Drôle d'amitié' demonstrates the extent to which Nizan's exit from the PCF and ensuing death exercised a particularly potent fascination over Sartre between 1940 and 1949, a fascination that was both personal and political.

Despite, therefore, the complicating factor of Nizan's ideological commitment to communism, there unquestionably existed a deep-rooted and genuine affinity on Sartre's part towards Nizan. This affinity was based on underlying psychological similarities which are at the root of the intermeshing between the personal and the social in the Nizan Affair of 1947. Jean Cau, Sartre's secretary between 1946 and 1957, has characterized the nature of Sartre's interpersonal relationships in the following terms:

> With Sartre there was no reconciliation after breaking off relations with Merleau-Ponty, with the first editorial team of *Les Temps Modernes*, with Aron ... He was *sectarian* in his approach, and did not hesitate to excommunicate people. There was in his character a kind of intellectual *imperialism* and *totalitarianism* ... Sartre was surprisingly *macho* in his relationships with men ... There was nothing feminine about Sartre in his dealings with men. There were direct confrontatations and heated exchanges. (my italics)[10]

Sectarian, imperialistic, totalitarian, macho: these are, according to Cau, the defining characteristics of Sartre's relationship with his intellectual peers, who were principally men.[11]

There are two conclusions that I would like to draw from Cau's remarks, one linked to Nizan, the other to the PCF. In the first instance, the same terms – sectarian, imperialistic and totalitarian – would define very precisely Nizan's own attitude to his intellectual peers in the 1930s. One need only read *Aden Arabie* (1931), *Les Chiens de garde* (1932), 'Littérature révolutionnaire en France' (1932), for example, to be convinced of Nizan's fundamentally sectarian mentality. Admittedly, the tone of Nizan's writings mellowed after 1934 in the run-up to the Popular Front and under the influence of the policy of '*La main tendue*' ('the outstretched hand'). Overall, however, Nizan's psychological perception of the world was resolutely Manichaean. He categorised his intellectual peers into two distinct groups: comrades-in-arms or ideological enemies. In this respect he displays a striking resemblance to Sartre's own psychological outlook as defined by Cau. It is not surprising that both Nizan and Sartre were fatally attracted to the PCF at historical moments when the party itself was at its most isolated and on the defensive, Nizan in 1928–9, Sartre in 1949–50.

The second conclusion that I would like to draw from Cau's remarks regarding the Sartre–Nizan relationship concerns the PCF. Their affinities to one another, both emotionally and temperamentally, have already been emphasised. However, it is important to stress the extent to which psychologically (particularly in Nizan's case) they were attracted to the imperialistic, sectarian structure of a communist party envisaged as the agency of violent social revolution. In other words, and I shall return to this later, despite their natural affinities one to another, they both had, to differing degrees, affinities with a notionally anti-capitalist, revolutionary communist party at different stages in its development. In Nizan's case, the ten years he spent within the party speak for themselves. In Sartre's case, the close 'fellow-travelling' relationship between 1950 and 1956 are significant and have a bearing on the interpretation of the Nizan Affair of 1947.[12]

NIZAN AND THE PCF: 1939–56

The origin of the Nizan Affair was, of course, Nizan's resignation from the PCF. The Nazi–Soviet pact of non-aggression was signed by Ribbentrop and Molotov on 23 August 1939. On 17 September the Soviet Union invaded Poland. On 25 September Nizan resigned from the PCF. The *manner* of his resignation was interpreted by members of the party as a highly provocative gesture. He had neither remained diplomatically silent, nor had he made any attempt to explain in public the reasons for his resignation. He had, however, chosen to publicise his act of departure, and this public disavowal, coinciding as it did with a ferocious government crackdown, was inevitably interpreted as a treacherous stab in the back that could not go unavenged.[13]

Vengeance was swift and brutal. In March 1940, two months prior to Nizan's death, Thorez launched a bitter attack on what he contemptuously designated as

> the handful of wretched deserters ... cowards and weaklings, spies and *agents-provocateurs* [who] had abandoned the position of the working class for that of the imperialists and planned to turn [the] fight for peace by the side of the Soviet Union into a policy of supporting the imperialist war-mongering of the French bourgeoisie.[14]

Thorez's denunciation was clearly designed to stiffen the resolve of party militants at a moment of extreme difficulty and danger when the party was being attacked on all sides. The tone of the entire piece is antagonistically defensive and draws heavily on Leninist–Stalinist first principles, stressing the need both for the party to 'cleanse itself by shaking off all traitors, opportunists and capitulators', and for the leadership to be uncompromisingly severe to the enemies of the party and the working class.[15]

Thorez presents Nizan unequivocally as such a traitor, opportunist and capitulator against whom the party must defend itself. Branded a 'police spy', Nizan was pilloried on two counts: first, for spreading the pernicious doctrine of 'National Communism', that is, communism in word and nationalism in deed;[16] second, for enacting in the reality of his life the treachery and cowardice portrayed in the fiction of his literature. Nizan, Thorez notes,

> has been satisfied to play in real life the wretched part of Pluvinage, the police spy he brings into his latest novel ... He has earned special laurels in the salons where cynicism and shamelessness are the marks of distinction.[17]

Despite the total absence of the merest shred of evidence that Nizan had betrayed the PCF in any sense other than resigning from the party itself, an orchestrated campaign to blacken his name was set in motion. Rumours began to circulate that Nizan had informed on his former comrades to the Ministry of the Interior, and these accusations of spying and betrayal were finally expressed in print by Henri Lefebvre in his highly polemical piece, 'L'Existentialisme', of 1946.[18] They were subsequently transposed into fictional form by Aragon in *Les Communistes* in 1949,[19] and by Simone Téry in *Beaux enfants qui n'hésitez pas* in 1957.[20] Even as recently as 1979, Henriette Nizan was still defending her husband's name against insinuations made by Roger Garaudy.[21]

It is important to establish that the origin of the accusations against Nizan was the 1940 tract written by Thorez. As has been extensively documented in the work by Rossi,[22] this tract was the direct result of a policy decision articulated by Georges Dimitrov, General Secretary of the Communist International, in October 1939: the defence of the nation state and the anti-fascist nature of the war were rejected as opportunism; 'revolutionary defeatism' as practised by the Bolsheviks in 1914–18 became the new party line.[23] After the events of 1939–40, therefore, given the publicity attached to Nizan's resignation from the party, given his failure to explain and publicly justify his actions, a failure compounded by his death, given the extremely difficult situation in which the party found itself and the inevitable tendency within its ranks to accept a disciplined, sectarian, defensive posture based on the idea of 'revolutionary defeatism', given the almost instinctive reaction of Lefebvre and Aragon to settle accounts with Nizan both personal and political, there is a certain inevitability about Nizan's fate in the wartime and postwar period. Once the original accusations had been levelled, they simply became part of the general socio-political discourse of the time. As long as the party felt threatened by external pressures, as long as it felt the need to justify and defend itself in polemical dispute, ineluctably the case of Nizan became an element in the polemic. After 1940 Nizan existed solely as a metaphor for communist renegade. The precise significance attached to this metaphor depended on the socio-political conjuncture of the time, whether it be 1947, 1960 or 1968.

SARTRE AND THE PCF: 1941–56

To examine the relationship between Sartre and the PCF between 1941 and 1956 is to get to the heart of the postwar intellectual climate in France. Sartre's attitude to the PCF progressed from ambivalence and antagonism (1941–9), to uncritical and enthusiastic support (1950–6), to open hostility and repudiation (post-1956). It is particularly important to establish the precise nature of the relationship between 1941 and 1947, since the Nizan Affair can only be properly understood as a facet of this ideological and political development.

When Sartre returned to France in late 1941, having escaped from a German prisoner-of-war camp in Trier, he attempted to make contact with the communist resistance group, but was rebuffed on the grounds that anyone who successfully escaped from a camp was not entirely above suspicion.[24] The suspicions surrounding Sartre's wartime role persist even today, and stand as a counterpoint to the suspicions surrounding Nizan's activities in 1939–40. For example, in a reassessment of Sartre entitled 'Sartre: The Suspect Witness', George Steiner is quick to point up what he perceives as inconsistencies between Sartre's words and Sartre's deeds during the war and Occupation.[25] However, by early 1943, he had been invited to join the CNE (*Comité National des Ecrivains*) and was contributing to the communist-run *Les Lettres Françaises*. At the Liberation Sartre was unquestionably sympathetic to the party that had been the backbone of the resistance, the '*parti des fusillés*'.

Between 1945 and 1947, however, the relationship between Sartre and the PCF became curiously tense and problematical. The underlying problem was that, unlike Nizan, Sartre refused to become a member of the party, preferring instead the fellow-travelling route. Given Sartre's spectacular rise to celebrity status in 1945, given the particular attractiveness of Sartrean existentialism to the younger generation of the period, the traditional recruiting ground of the PCF, it is not surprising that opposition to Sartre emerged from within the ranks of the party itself. The publication in 1943 of *L'Etre et le néant* had offered an alternative philosophical system to Marxism, and the launch in 1945 of *Les Temps Modernes* offered an alternative cultural and political forum to *Les Lettres françaises* and the CNE. Despite its enormous resistance prestige as '*le parti des fusillés*', therefore, the PCF was progressively upstaged by a more libertarian, existentialist group that was, in particular, siphoning off potential recruits and diverting attention from what the party judged to be the real political agenda of the time. Although there were early skirmishes between Sartre and the PCF in 1945 and 1946, in particular Roger Garaudy's attack on Sartre in *Les Lettres françaises* of 1945,[26] and Sartre's critique of what he referred to as 'scholastic Marxism' or the 'Stalinist neo-Marxism of the time in 'Matérialisme et révolution' in 1946,[27] matters came to a head only in 1947–8, coinciding precisely with the Nizan affair.

What is significant here is that in the same way that Nizan's fate in 1940 had been sealed at the international level by the decision reached in October 1939 by Dimitrov to adopt the imperialist war thesis and advocate 'revolutionary defeatism', so in a similar vein Sartre's fate in the postwar period (and, by extension, Nizan's) was sealed by a decision taken at the international level. At the first meeting of the Cominform in September 1947, the official view of the Cold War was laid down when Zhdanov announced: 'The USA has proclaimed a new, openly predatory and expansionist orientation, with the aim of world-wide domination'.[28] Just as Thorez, Lefebvre and Aragon had adopted and embroidered upon Dimitrov's policy statements in 1940, so the process of political and ideological embroidery was taken up in the postwar situation by Thorez, Kanapa and Casanova.

It is important to dwell on the process whereby the political impact of the Cold War situation at the international level was filtered down and embedded itself in the matrix of French national politics. At the Communist Party Congress of 25 June 1947 Thorez noted: 'Financial oligarchies can maintain their dominant position only by corrupting the mind, by reducing it to impotence through the cult of individualism and through intellectual anarchy.'[29] The implication of Thorez's remarks is that in 1947 the PCF must wage a war on the ideological and intellectual front in order to win over the hearts and minds of the French people. In other words, '*le parti des fusillés*', having emerged victorious from a clandestine military war against an occupying force, was now called upon to wage an overt intellectual war against those individuals and groups who were corrupting the minds of the populace at large and thereby serving the interests of the forces of reaction.

Laurent Casanova, for example, in a revealing analogy, equates the literature of the American novelist Henry Miller with the atomic bomb: 'Miller's literature is a by-product of the atomic bomb. Unlike the atomic bomb, however, it is an export product designed to spread confusion and cause panic outside America.'[30] In a Cold War situation, where the Soviet Union felt threatened by an awe-inspiring American nuclear capability, literature and ideas became the weapons of battle. Artists and intellectuals on both sides of the political divide were driven remorselessly into ideological combat. In particular, Communist Party artists and intellectuals felt compelled to wage war against the latest manifestation of bourgeois ideology, existentialism.[31] The PCF's deliberate assault on the alleged decadence and depravity not only of Sartrean existentialism but also of American writers such as Henry Miller was the logical, inevitable consequence of an international Cold War situation in which the French Communist Party, despite its residual prestige as '*le parti des fusillés*', felt threatened on all sides: in May the communist ministers were dismissed from the Ramadier government, in June details of the Marshall aid plan were announced, in September the Cominform banned communist parties from participating in national governments (admonishing in particular the PCF's previous involvement in government during 1946 and 1947), and in October the Gaullist movement won a landslide victory in the municipal elections. The PCF consequently chose to defend itself in a progressively more hostile, belligerent and provocative manner.

In retrospect, it is hardly surprising that Sartre's own literary and political attacks on the PCF in 1947 and 1948 (*Qu'est-ce que la littérature?*[32] and the *Temps Modernes* radio broadcasts[33]) were rebuffed head-on by the party's intellectuals, specifically Jean Kanapa, one of Sartre's former pupils, in *L'Existentialisme n'est pas un humanisme.*[34] Kanapa's efforts to denigrate existentialism as the corrupting ideology of an oppressive class, and to malign Sartre personally as the disciple of the Nazi sympathiser Heidegger, merely underline the polarised nature of the political and cultural climate of the time. From 1948 open warfare existed between Sartre and the PCF. Only in 1950, with the outbreak of the Korean War, would hostilities between Sartre and the PCF come temporarily to a halt, ushering in a period of close co-operation that would last until the Soviet invasion of Hungary in 1956.

SARTRE AND THE NIZAN AFFAIR

The preceding analysis offers an overarching political, ideological and cultural context to the Nizan Affair. I now intend finally to focus directly on the Affair itself, clarifying the precise chronology of events, emphasising particularly the linkages between the Resistance and Cold War mentalities, as well as the interaction between the personal and ideological strands of the Sartre–Nizan relationship.

Rumours of Nizan's alleged treachery had been circulating in communist circles since 1940. In 1946, Henri Lefebvre brought matters to a head when he published his slanderous attack on Nizan in his book entitled *L'Existentialisme*. Lefebvre's assertions prompted Sartre and twenty-five other well-known intellectuals[35] to spring to Nizan's defence and publish a statement in April 1947 seeking to establish the falsity of the rumours, explicitly implicating Aragon, and demanding immediate proof of Nizan's alleged treachery.[36] The tone of the statement was deliberately provocative. So provocative, in fact, that Louis Martin-Chauffier, a friend of Nizan, but also President of the CNE, felt unable to sign the statement, despite his sympathy with the motives underlying it.[37] On 11 April the CNE responded, disdainfully rejecting the aggressive manner in which the protest had been made, and arguing that its principal aim was not to clear Nizan's name but rather to discredit Aragon, and by implication the CNE itself.[38] Sartre then raised the stakes further, declaring that the allegations of Nizan's treachery had been made to him personally by Aragon; rather than engaging in diversionary tactics, Aragon and Lefebvre should either substantiate their claims or withdraw them.[39] Both Aragon and Lefebvre refused to be implicated further, with the result that Nizan's innocence was proclaimed in the July number of *Les Temps Modernes* as the necessary conclusion to be drawn from the silence of the communist slanderers.[40]

The extent of communist hostility and aggressiveness at the time needs to be registered. The polemic was not really about Nizan at all. It was principally about the increasingly besieged state of the PCF, with the attendant necessity on the part of communist intellectuals of the time to ward off every attack with vituperative counter-attacks. Claude Morgan, for example, drawing an analogy between the full-scale anti-communist offensive under way in the United States and current political manoeuvres in France, sought to defend his party's name not only by casting aspersions on the motives of those defending Nizan, but also by denigrating Nizan himself in pointedly personal terms:

> I knew Nizan personally. I did not like him because he was a cold character, jealous above all of his own reputation.

> His public repudiation of his party and his comrades, at the moment when they were persecuted and in danger, filled me with disgust.[41]

In similar vein, Guy Leclerc, incensed by what he perceived as a wholly unjustified attack on his party, responded with a venomous denunciation of those using the Nizan Affair as a convenient pretext to undermine the PCF:

> Brice PARAIN, dismissed from *L'Humanité* because he was Editor of a police newspaper, *Détective*; André BRETON, a former guest of Trotsky, the most important servant of the international Political Police against the workers' movement … Jean PAULHAN, the man for whom Romain Rolland was a traitor by the same title as Alphonse de CHATEAUBRIANT; Henri JEANSON, founder and editor of the Nazi newspaper *Aujourd'hui*. And a host of others who do not seem uncomfortable in the company of these 'specialists'.[42]

In the polarised ideological climate of 1947 dispassionate assessments were impossible. Those involved were forced to take sides either for or against the PCF. There simply was no middle ground. Pierre Daix, commenting in 1990 on the vituperative political and cultural climate of 1947, the moment when Kanapa launched a bitter attack in Pierre Seghers's *Poésie 47* against American literature, against Sartre, against Paulhan, remarks: 'Somehow we associated ourselves with it without really believing in it … ; we thought at that time that we should act through *loyalty* to the party' (my italics).[43] Daix, in other words, alleges that he did not believe in the Cold War cultural assault being carried out at the time by Kanapa, Casanova, Aragon *et alia*, but went along with it through a sense of duty to the party. His words betray a sense of powerlessness experienced by one individual enmeshed within the party machine. Evidently, he is retrospectively attempting to distance himself from the worse excesses of Communist Party cultural policy in 1947. There is nonetheless a genuine sense here in which the PCF internal organisation literally asphyxiated alternative views. Democratic centralism eliminated debate. Kanapa had been specifically assigned to cultural matters. Daix, although harbouring misgivings, kept his head down, turned a blind eye, partly for reasons of duty to the party, but partly also for reasons of self-preservation within the party.

This mixture of retrospective self-justification and uneasy party allegiance emerges forcefully in Daix's account of the Nizan Affair, which merits quotation in full:

> Of all the representatives of communist ideas at that time, I undoubtedly felt closest to Nizan ... I was not dismayed when I learned that he had broken with the PCF in September 1939; the Nazi–Soviet pact was not an issue for my generation. We believed that it was a tactic of war ... It became a problem for me at the beginning of the Occupation because we had to distribute a leaflet in August–September 1940 which denounced Nizan as a traitor ... At the time, since treachery was something which did occur ... it was not iniquitous to think that Nizan had betrayed the party ... When I returned from the camp, I met Henriette Nizan, and, as far as I was concerned, there was no shadow of a doubt ... if Nizan had been called a traitor, it was not because he was an informer or a cop, but because he had rejected the Nazi–Soviet pact. If you like, it was a political disagreement.
>
> I discussed the matter with Aragon towrds the middle of the 1950s. Aragon said to me: 'You understand, it is the leadership of the party that has decided this', and he spoke of the matter as if it had been Duclos. After Sartre had written the preface to *Aden Arabie* in 1960, I said to Aragon 'the only way to settle the Nizan Affair is for me to write a review of Sartre's preface'... And I came back to the task in 1969, after the events of May 1968. I said to Aragon: 'There is no reason not to carry out the necessary self-criticism in this Affair'.

> And Aragon replied: 'You cannot do that. Duclos is standing as a candidate for President of the Republic. You must understand that it would bring down our newspaper'.
>
> I am saying all this because I had throughout all this time been convinced that the author of Nizan the traitor had been Duclos. When I wrote my biography of Aragon whilst he was still alive, that is to say in 1975, I said to myself: 'I must shed light on the Nizan Affair. Where did it originate? Who said that Nizan was a traitor?' That is when I discovered that Nizan had been called a traitor for the first time in a relatively unknown pamphlet, *The Communist International*, which was edited in Scandinavia and signed by Thorez. I published this in my biography of Aragon without any response from Aragon or Lefebvre.[44]

Although Daix asserts that Nizan was the communist with whom intellectually he had the most in common, and that Nizan's betrayal of the party amounted in his eyes to no more than a political disagreement over the Nazi–Soviet pact, he implicitly concedes his failure to do anything whatsoever about rehabilitating Nizan's name until the mid-1950s. His account of the role of Aragon, Duclos and Thorez, if taken at face value, demonstrates not only the duplicitous nature of Aragon, but also the totally inadequate level of information within the party itself. Daix's lengthy explanation of the manner in which he discovered the role of Maurice Thorez in the Nizan Affair is to some extent almost pitiable. Admittedly, he is engaging here in a strategy of retrospective self-exoneration, but nonetheless to claim to be ignorant of the role of Thorez, given the extensive documentation of the facts by Rossi in 1948 and 1951, is quite breathtaking. The difficulty, of course, is that Rossi himself, formerly Angelo Tasca, a prominent member of the Italian Communist Party and the Communist International until his expulsion in 1929, was a collaborator under Vichy. Consequently, his record of the actions of the

PCF during the Phoney War would doubtless have been automatically rejected as anti-communist propaganda fabricated by a fascist collaborator, unworthy of the attention of a party steeped in its Resistance mythology as *'le parti des fusillés'*.

The issue of Resistance and Collaboration was in many ways the sub-text of the Nizan Affair. It is highly significant that the party chose to defend itself throughout this postwar period in Resistance terminology. In 1947, with the expulsion of the communist ministers from the Ramadier government, with the onset of the Cold War, the party felt threatened in similar fashion to 1939 in the aftermath of the Nazi–Soviet pact and its subsequent outlawing. It felt the need to go underground, the need to revive its wartime resistance, subversive role. Auguste Lecoeur has recalled a conversation with Maurice Thorez in 1947 during which he was explicitly instructed to re-establish the PCF as an illegal organisation, a consequence of the decisions previously taken at the Cominform summit in September of that year.[45] Equally, although it is undoubtedly true that the specific historical conjuncture of 1947 prompted a return to the Resistance mentality, it is also the case that the party itself was both tactically and morally wedded to the idea of perpetuating the Resistance myth and the Resistance outlook.

This latter point was graphically illustrated, for example, in the Paulhan Affair of the same year. The issue at stake was the *liste noire* of writers, artists and intellectuals who in the view of the CNE had collaborated with the German Occupying force. Jean Paulhan, who had been one of the instigators of *Les Lettres françaises* and of the CNE itself, argued a case for removing specific individuals from the proscribed list on the grounds that writers in the public domain had the right to be wrong in their political judgements, citing in particular the case of Rimbaud in 1873 and Romain Rolland in 1914.[46] The CNE response was predictably hostile, asserting the need to keep a watchful eye on the writings of those who had betrayed France at her hour of need, refusing to accept Paulhan's slurs on the intellectual probity of Rimbaud and Rolland,[47] and asserting its right to ostracise writers who had collaborated during the Occupation. The parallels with the Nizan Affair are quite striking. In both cases the issue at stake was the retribution to be meted out to those who had simultaneously betrayed France and the PCF. The fact that the interests of France and the interests of the PCF were frequently incompatible (as in 1939 at the moment of the Nazi–Soviet pact, and in 1947 at the moment of the outbreak of the Cold War) is strategically glossed over by careful exploitation of the unifying myth of the French Resistance embodied in the courage of the communist partisans defending *la patrie*.

In essence Paulhan was advocating the need to separate the cultural sphere from the political sphere. In his eyes, writers should be accountable solely for actions that contravened the law, and should not consequently be punished for the ideological slant of their writings. It went entirely against the grain of Paulhan's liberal, democratic views for a self-elected group of writers to make public moral judgements on those writers who had collaborated, to act as literary executioners by preventing the publication of their work, to function as guardians of public morals defending the interests of '*la patrie*', particularly when the accusers were in his opinion potential collaborators themselves, as ready to welcome possible Soviet intervention in France then as fascist sympathisers had been ready to welcome Nazi intervention in France in 1940.[48]

The intriguing point, as Jean Pouillon has corroborated,[49] is that Sartre did not share Paulhan's liberal views. The postwar Sartrean vision of commitment necessitated placing literature at the centre of social activity. Writers are responsible for their words and their acts. Literature is the point of mediation between writer and public, not a sanitised cultural product distanced from political and social reality. Sartre's uncompromising, imperialistic, almost totalitarian frame of mind matched precisely the mood of the time – judgemental, accusing, ethically-positioned. The essay on Baudelaire written in 1946–7 is a classic exemplification of

Sartre's postwar perception of the need to be harshly critical, unequivocally censorious when assessing the moral stance of writers during and after the war. And, as has already been noted, Nizan during the 1930s unquestionably shared this view, and would probably have inclined towards the brutal judgements of his erstwhile communist comrades and Sartre himself, rather than the more accommodating Paulhan.

We are left, then, with this enormous paradox. In 1947 Sartre could not defend Nizan in the same way that Paulhan could have done, from an accommodating, liberal perspective.[50] His imperialistic, sectarian temperament ruled out this possibility. Sartre was consequently forced into a contradictory stance. In the preface to *Aden Arabie* he recalls the ambiguity of his actions, particularly at the moment when he appeared to have silenced his communist detractors: 'Our victory frightened us: *deep down we loved these unjust soldiers of justice*' (my italics).[51] Despite the ferocious personal attacks levelled against himself by the PCF in 1947, despite the crass and unjustified campaign of calumny and vilification mounted by the PCF against his best friend, Sartre acknowledges an underlying sympathy for those whom he refers to as 'unjust soldiers of Justice'. He committed himself to Nizan as far as he could, but instinctively did not overstep the mark. At one level, he was held back by an implicit disapproval of Nizan's apparent allegiance to the Stalinist mentality of the PCF during the 1930s. At another level, sensing that his future itinerary would be as a fellow traveller with these 'unjust soldiers', he did not overstate his criticisms of a party towards which, despite everything, he felt a certain attraction.[52]

And yet, although Sartre concluded retrospectively that he had failed to do justice to Nizan in 1947, thwarted as he had been by an unfavourable socio-political climate, there remains a striking testimony to Sartre's innermost feelings embodied in the description of the characters of Brunet and Schneider/Vicarios in 'Drôle d'amitié'.[53] 'Drôle d'amitié' ('A Strange Kind of Friendship'), published for the first time in *Les Temps Modernes* in November and December 1949, is a tantalising fragment of a novel where Sartre draws the line emotionally on his relationship with Nizan. Vicarios, dying in Brunet's arms during an abortive attempt to escape from a German prisoner-of-war camp, speaks volumes on the Sartre–Nizan relationship. This fictional death of Nizan is a strangely appropriate epitaph to the intertwining of the ideological and the personal in their friendship:

> [Brunet] knew that Vicarios was going to die: despair and hatred were working their way back along the course of this wasted life, eating it away at birth. No human victory could take away this absolute of suffering: it was the Party that was killing him; even if the USSR were to win, men are alone. Brunet bent down, plunged his hand in Vicarios's dirty hair, shouted as if he could still save him from the horror of it all, as if two men who were done for could, at the last minute, overcome solitude:
>
> 'I don't give a damn about the Party: you are my only friend.'
>
> Vicarios did not hear, his mouth gurgled bitterly and blew bubbles, whilst Brunet shouted in the wind:
>
> 'My only friend!'[54]

CONCLUSION

The Nizan Affair is a complex amalgam of personal, ideological and political issues. Both Nizan and Sartre experienced the bitterness of the realisation that genuine friendship and political comradeship were incompatible within the ranks of the PCF. As André Pierrard, a close associate of Auguste Lecoeur during the 1940s and 1950s, was reluctantly forced to conclude, the inner workings of the leadership of the PCF frequently resembled gang warfare, where individuals competed one with another for supremacy and sought to eliminate dangerous rivals in order to pre-empt being eliminated themselves.[55] How poignant to recall that during the 1930s Nizan proudly and publicly differentiated between what he perceived as the moral integrity of the international diplomacy of the Communist Party and the fascist politics of Hitlerism based explicitly on the lawless brutality of gang warfare.[56] How revealing to hear Auguste Lecoeur himself, at one time a serious contender for the leadership of the PCF, declare: 'I would never have trusted anybody in the secretariat of the Central Committee of the party'.[57] How sad to hear Claude Morgan, a prime-mover in the creation of *Les Lettres Françaises*, ask rhetorically in 1969:

> Is the Party destined to continue to practice this untenable Stalinist method which consists in eliminating from history those comrades or friends who no longer follow its political line at a given moment? ... how can the Party hope to be influential and display such heartlessness?[58]

Sartre himself was sufficiently far-sighted in 1948 to have asserted that 'the Stalinist community with its power to excommunicate remains present in love and friendship which are relations between individual people'.[59] The Cold War prevented Sartre from doing justice to Nizan during the post-Liberation period. Individual moral conscience was eclipsed by political expediency. An anti-collaborationist, '*épuration*' ('purge') mentality became fused with a sectarian, Cold War mentality, and Sartre and Nizan were trapped in the middle. The result was that the Nizan Affair fizzled out like a damp squid. Nothing seemed to have been definitively resolved. Nizan was not to be properly rehabilitated until 1960, when Sartre's flirtation with the French Communist Party was at an end.

5

Sartre and the Politics of Violence: Maoism in the Aftermath of May 1968

'Violence', noted Sartre in 1960 in *Critique de la raison dialectique*, 'must be defined as a structure of human action under the sway of Manichaeism and in a context of scarcity'.[1] In other words, in societies in which scarcity predominates, that is to say where insufficient material resources are available to satisfy the needs of the population as a whole, human relations are based on what he refers to as 'negative reciprocity'. The Other is a constant threat to the self insofar as the Other constitutes a human agent capable of outmanoeuvring and undermining my projects, my efforts to sustain my own existence at a material level in a world of scarcity. The presence of the Other accordingly represents a permanent threat of deprivation and death not only to my material being, but also to my very humanity insofar as it forces me to retaliate, to engage in a process of counter-violence, to wage war against the Other perceived as an external danger to myself, to destroy the inhuman project of the Other, and in so doing constitute in my own self the inhumanity of the Other.

This dialectical process of antagonistic and hostile social relations in which inhuman actions of violence are motivated in a context of scarcity, and consequently summon up retaliatory inhuman actions as counter-violence, is described by Sartre as follows:

> Nothing – not even wild beasts or microbes – could be more terrifying for man than a species which is intelligent,

> carnivorous and cruel, and which can understand and outwit human intelligence, and whose aim is precisely the destruction of man. This, however, is obviously our own species as perceived in others by each of its members in the context of scarcity.
>
> Thus man is *objectively* constituted as non-human, and this non-humanity is expressed in *praxis* by the perception of evil as the structure of the Other ... But this *violence of the Other* is not an objective reality except in the sense that it exists in all men as the universal motivation of counter-violence; it is nothing but the unbearable fact of broken reciprocity and of the systematic exploitation of man's humanity for the destruction of the human. Counter-violence is exactly the same thing, but as a process of restoration, as a response to a provocation: if I destroy the non-humanity of the anti-human in my adversary, I cannot help destroying the humanity of man in him, and realising his non-humanity in myself. I may try to kill, to torture, to enslave, or simply to mystify, but in any case my aim will be to eliminate alien freedom as a hostile force, a force which can expel me from the practical field and make me into a 'surplus man' condemned to death.[2]

This initial theorising on the nature and origins of violence in human societies (scarcity, negative reciprocity, violence, counter-violence) is taken a step further in the second volume of the *Critique* insofar as Sartre adds a political value-judgement to his argument. The object of analysis in this instance is the physically violent 'sport' of boxing.[3] Although Sartre's principal concern in this analysis is the attempt to demonstrate the dialectical unity of history through the assertion that any particular boxing match incarnates, singularises, not only all boxing, but also all violence mediated by the structures of a class-driven bourgeois society, what is of interest for my purposes in this analysis is the value-judgement attached to his theorising.

Starting from the premise that 'bourgeois boxing must be studied on the basis of the real structures of the exploitative system',[4] Sartre interprets the sport of boxing as a bourgeois domestification of proletarian class violence. The boxing promoter commodifies the violence of a working-class boxer for consumption within the economic structures of bourgeois society. Consequently, the political dimension of proletarian class violence is neutralised through alienation within the framework of a specific economic system. The violence of the working-class boxer is converted from 'a wild and liberating passion' into 'a painful and dangerous labour'.[5] Sartre's own value-judgements are here publicly visible. The neutralised, commodified violence of bourgeois boxing is politically of little interest, since it merely symbolises the exploitative structures of an oppressive bourgeois society. The 'wild and liberating passion' of an emancipatory class violence, on the other hand, holds the key in Sartre's system to political liberation. Ultimately, it is the politically liberating force of class violence that remains a constant in the theory and practice of Sartre's politics.

Sartre remained convinced throughout his life that violence was unquestionably justified during periods of revolutionary transformation, notably at those precarious moments when the revolutionary impetus was itself in jeopardy. He forcefully articulated this belief in the need for revolutionary violence in an interview with Michel-Antoine Burnier in 1973:

> In a revolutionary country in which the bourgeoisie has been driven from power, those members of the bourgeoisie who might seek to stir up discontent would deserve the death sentence. Not that I would harbour the slightest animosity towards them. It is natural that the forces of reaction act in their own interest. But a revolutionary regime must rid itself of those individuals who threaten it and I see no means other than death. It is always possible to escape from prison. *The revolutionaries of 1793 probably did not kill enough* and as a consequence

> facilitated a return to order, then to the Restoration… I am of course opposed to anything which resembles the Moscow trials. *But the revolution implies violence and the existence of a more radical party which imposes itself at the expense of other more conciliatory groups.* (my italics)[6]

This is an unequivocal statement. The revolutionaries of 1793 did not, in Sartre's view, kill enough counter-revolutionaries. In a revolutionary state, violence is not only a legitimate but a necessary weapon of social transformation. It is, of course, important to stress that Sartre is referring to a *distant* revolutionary state, distant insofar as it is either a purely hypothetical example, or else a past historical event. In other words, he is articulating a course of action that would pertain in a situation other than contemporary France. The invocation of the discourse of violent revolutionary change is therefore facilitated by this historical and social *distance*.

There is, as I have argued in Chapter 4 of this book,[7] an underlying sectarian, authoritarian strand in Sartre's thinking, which co-exists paradoxically with a fundamentally libertarian and anarchistic outlook on life. Jean Cau has referred to this tendency as a sectarian desire on Sartre's part for confrontation with his intellectual adversaries,[8] an attitude that emphasises conflictual violence rather than empathetic conciliation. Sartre's temperamental affinity for discourses of violent revolutionary change was undoubtedly at the root of his fascination for the distant revolutionary struggles in the Soviet Union, Cuba, Algeria and Vietnam, particularly following the accession to power of de Gaulle in 1958, when the revolutionary impetus in France seemed to have been extinguished. Sartre assesses the role of violence in postwar international politics in the following terms:

> A socialist has no choice but to be violent because he sets out to achieve an end that the ruling class totally rejects: this appeared to be taken for granted in 1950. Khrushchev arrived on the scene and laid the foundations of 'peaceful co-existence', which amounted to privileging revisionism.

> Then de Gaulle seized power in France and the parties of the left were crushed. Nobody spoke any more of violence. The left remained silent in the expectation that an electoral victory would give it power through peaceful means. In the 1960s, you could not mention the healthy principle of revolutionary violence without being called an intellectual adventurer: 58–68 were years that must be spoken of in all modesty. And then violence revealed itself and consumed the whole of France.[9]

It is consequently clear that Sartre accepted revolutionary violence as a legitimate and necessary part of left-wing political action. The originality of the events of May 1968 is that they offered Sartre a unique opportunity to test his theoretical views on violence and revolutionary praxis against the social reality of contemporary France. As Sartre himself frequently asserted, May 68 constituted a watershed in his development insofar as the radical ideas of May directly challenged the underlying beliefs of both traditional left-wing politics and of the intellectual class itself. The objective of the following analysis is therefore to examine Sartre's involvement in the revolutionary politics that emerged from the events of May 68, focusing specifically on his attitude towards revolutionary violence. Sartre's links with *La Gauche Prolétarienne* (GP), as well as with revolutionary publications such as *La Cause du Peuple, J'Accuse, La Cause du Peuple–J'Accuse* and *Libération* will accordingly be assessed in order to determine the extent to which the fundamental transformation that Sartre underwent in the aftermath of May 68 constituted an act of faith in the violence of terrorist acts or merely a continuing allegiance to the verbal violence of words. At the same time, Sartre's views on the role of a revolutionary press will be presented as a reflection of his views on the function and limits of revolutionary violence in the France of the 1970s.

Although Sartre's postwar political itinerary in ideological and tactical terms is essentially the story of his relationship with Marxism and the PCF, it is also at a more personal, individual level, the record of a quest for a political community within which to work. Even during the early 1950s, at the time when Sartre uncritically endorsed the PCF in 'Les Communistes et la Paix', he was never entirely above the suspicion of party intellectuals and militants alike. His close friendship during the 1930s with the 'traitor' Nizan, and the postwar polemic between Sartre's existentialist group and the PCF, had sown too many seeds of distrust for there to be any sense of total reconciliation. It is generally recognised, moreover, that Sartre's relations with the PCI and Togliatti, in particular, were much more friendly than with the PCF and Thorez. The absence of a genuine political community in Sartre's life prior to 1968 cannot therefore be overestimated. What attracted Sartre to the post-68 Maoist groups was not simply their political energy and imagination, but also their comradeship, their readiness to accept Sartre on his own terms within their political community, despite fundamental differences of opinion between them in terms of ideology and strategy.

The particularly intriguing aspect of Sartre's encounter with the GP and the post-1968 revolutionary press was that, for the first time outside the context of Third World struggles, Sartre discovered a political community that was potentially more radical and more violent than himself, and that as a consequence he was forced to confront the *reality* of revolutionary violence rather than its distant revolutionary image. It is the nature of this negotiation between Sartre and Maoist politics that I would now like to address, focusing initially on Sartre's attitude to different kinds of revolutionary violence, subsequently on the relationship between revolutionary violence and the revolutionary press.

SARTRE AND MAOIST VIOLENCE

A close reading of Sartre's political writings of this period reveals a clear distinction on his part between forms of violence that he considers both justifiable and useful in France, and those which he judges to be pointless and counter-productive. This differentiation might best be designated as a distinction between 'organic class violence' on the one hand, and 'abstract terrorist violence' on the other. Sartre distinguishes between violence that emerges organically as an act of class retaliation against the social exploitation carried out by the French ruling class (a 'wild and liberating passion'), and abstract terrorist violence that is not organically linked to, that does not have its roots in, the social community in whose name the violence is perpetrated. Organic class violence is, in Sartre's eyes, both legitimate and justifiable. Abstract terrorist violence, on the other hand, is of no value since it cannot ultimately serve the interests of a broad social community, but merely reflects the sectarian revolutionary views of an isolated terrorist group. The following examples illustrate this particular distinction.

In February 1970, following the death of 16 miners in a firedamp explosion in the north of France, several miners were arrested and accused of fire-bombing the offices of the mine management as an act of retaliation. Sartre's analysis of the events leading to this violent act of arson constitutes a lengthy account of the manner in which over many years the management had privileged productivity over safety in the mines. Consequently, it is Sartre's contention that the mine-owners are themselves ultimately guilty of the murder of the 16 miners who died in the firedamp explosion. Even were it to be proven, Sartre contends, that the miners themselves had carried out the fire-bombing, that action can be justified as an act of retaliatory class violence against a management group itself guilty of murder:

> The State as an employer is guilty of the murder of 4 February 1970. The management and the engineers responsible for pit no. 6 are its executors. They are consequently equally guilty of deliberate murder; they deliberately chose productivity rather than safety, that is to

> say they placed the production of *things* above human lives. The miners accused of having set light to the offices of the Coal-mines on Tuesday 17 February are not perhaps the instigators of this fire: so far nothing has been proven. In any case, those who did set fire to the offices merely expressed popular anger: they demonstrated the indignation of tens of thousands of workers who feel trapped, condemned to rapid death or to a slow death through silicosis ... if this special court were to condemn them, it would condemn all the miners of the north who for some time have been passing judgement on the situation and on the men who maintain it, and who after a recent similar catastrophe called the Minister Ortoli 'criminal' and 'assassin' when he came to the funeral.[10]

Sartre's underlying argument is crystal clear. Violent acts cannot be isolated from the social conditions which produce them. They are in this sense an organic expression of class consciousness at a given moment in time, and are consequently, in Sartre's eyes, morally justifiable. 'Everywhere that revolutionary violence originates in the masses, it is immediately and profoundly moral', notes Sartre.[11] The retaliatory violence of the working class merely mirrors the exploitative violence of a ruling élite and must be judged accordingly. It is therefore synonymous with what Sartre refers to in *Critique de la raison dialectique* as the phenomenon of 'counter-violence', a consequence of 'interiorised scarcity' and a 'response to a provocation'.[12] This discourse of justifiable and moral retaliatory class violence is a constant in Sartre's thinking throughout the 1970s: the government, the police, business and management élites, all are perceived as engaging in violence against the working class and hence become legitimate targets for the retaliatory violence of the working class itself.

Two points need to be made at the outset regarding Sartre's view of a justifiable and hence moral retaliatory class violence. The first is that by linking violent acts directly to the social conditions from which they arise, the precise nature of the violence itself is inevitably perceived as being shaped organically by the human agents and the social conditions which produce it. More specifically, the limits of retaliatory violence are imposed by the social environment from which the violence itself emerges. Hence, to speak of 'organic class violence' is not simply to assert that the agents of particular acts were members of one community rather than another, since the concept of 'membership' is fluid; specific individuals might belong to more than one group and the level of integration within a group is infinitely variable. Rather, violence is organic when it is informed and given shape by the inner will of a community, when the community as a whole recognises and accepts such violence as the embodiment of its own chosen destiny.

The second point is that, despite the polarised and Manichaean structure of the cycle of violence and counter-violence, Sartre is nonetheless arguing that the counter-violence instigated by oppressed communities is ultimately the means of establishing a profoundly moral society; that there is, in other words, a route to the human via the inhumanity of the retaliatory violence of the exploited and the oppressed.[13] Such a view is reflected in the ideas of the ex-Maiost, Daniel Rondeau, who has underlined the quasi-religious, saintly sentiment at the root of Maoist violence:

> I think that we in some ways resembled the monks of the Middle Ages who wished to demonstrate at any cost their poverty and humility, and who wanted to conquer heaven through violence... our desire for poverty and humility was so sincere that it resembled what in the past would have been religious sentiment.[14]

In the light of the preceding remarks, it is not surprising that abstract terrorist violence was rejected by Sartre as an inappropriate strategy for the France of the 1970s. The example of the militant Maoist reaction to the killing of

Pierre Overney in February 1972 is highly symbolic in this respect. On 8 March 1972, following the death of Overney at the gates of the Renault factory at Billancourt, and his subsequent funeral, an employment officer of the company, Robert Nogrette, was kidnapped by activists of the *Nouvelle Résistance Populaire* (NRP), the militant wing of the GP, as a retaliation against the assassination of Overney. It is important to stress that Sartre did not perceive this as an action emerging organically from a working-class community insofar as the death threat implied by the abduction appeared to exceed the nature of the oppression for which Nogrette himself was deemed to be symbolically responsible.

Liliane Siegel, the co-editor with Sartre of *La Cause du Peuple*, who twice appeared in court on charges of libel against Raymond Marcellin, the interior minister, was in Sartre's apartment on the very day that the kidnappers came to seek Sartre's advice after having seized Nogrette. Sartre's response, according to Liliane Siegel, was dismissive. She maintains that Sartre told them that they were faced with the stark choice of killing Nogrette or releasing him, that they should have asked for his advice before initiating such an action, and that after the event he had no advice to offer them.[15] Siegel alleges that Sartre would definitely *not* have supported the idea of the kidnapping, that he considered that it was a stupid political error, and that Sartre rejected terrorist acts of this kind as misguided and counter-productive in the France of the early 1970s. Simone de Beauvoir corroborates Liliane Siegel's version of events in *La Cérémonie des adieux*, asserting: 'Sartre did not approve of the abduction of Nogrette.'[16] It is, of course, worth noting with respect to the Nogrette incident not only that Nogrette was released unharmed, but also that (according to the ex-Maoist, Christian Jambet) the guns used by the Maoists in this incident were *not* loaded, through fear of killing anyone, and that the kidnapping is consequently most appropriately interpreted as a *symbolic* act of violence.[17]

Another telling example of Sartre's lack of sympathy for abstract terrorist violence in France relates to his visit in 1974 to Andreas Baader, the German terrorist jailed in Stammheim prison in Stuttgart. After seeing Baader, Sartre commented to the TV journalists outside the prison:

> There are different methods which enable the left to counter the forces that are opposed to left-wing movements, and [Baader's] is perhaps valid in Germany, I don't know, *but it will not succeed in France*. (my italics)[18]

As a footnote to the example of Andreas Baader, it is worth quoting the words of Jean-Pierre Le Dantec, the imprisoned editor of *La Cause du Peuple*, who remains convinced that Sartre's presence among the Maoists was an important factor in preventing them from stepping over the brink in terms of terrorist violence. In 1990 he affirmed:

> In a curious way Sartre's intervention saved us, in the sense that we could have gone very far in our commitment, including ending up in terrorism, as some others did at the time.[19]

The preceding examples demonstrate a fundamental differentiation in Sartre's thinking between on the one hand class violence that emerges organically from a social environment in which ruling groups violently exploit working-class communities for material gain, and on the other, abstract terrorist violence perpetrated by isolated sectarian groups not closely linked with those working-class communities. In other words, organic class violence is both morally justifiable and on occasions unavoidable, whereas sectarian terrorist acts are of little political value. Sartre succinctly summarised his position as follows:

> I support violence as a political weapon where it is necessary, that is to say where mass confrontations exist or can be unleashed ... but this does not mean that I consider

> violence like that of Baader, that is to say political assassination attempts carried out here and there in Germany, as a valid political act.[20]

It is perhaps worth dwelling briefly on this comparison between French and German terrorist violence of the time. In a Channel 4 television documentary centred on Silke Maier-Witt, a member of the Red Army Faction,[21] the German terrorist group responsible for the kidnapping and assassination in 1977 of West Germany's leading industrialist, Hanns-Martin Schleyer, and for the failed assassination attempt on General Alexander Haig in 1979, there emerged this paradoxical dialectic between self-proclaimed moral objectives based on the liberation of oppressed groups, and the inhuman violence and murder instigated in the name of such objectives. At one point in the documentary Maier-Witt remarks:

> It was awful enough that you really wanted to be like that, to kill somebody, to be able to kill somebody. *At the same time we thought that we would like to make the world a more human world.* (my italics)[22]

Chancellor Helmut Schmidt's televised response to such claims echoes curiously Sartre's insistence that in order to be justifiable, violence must be organically linked to the life-style of those in whose name it is being carried out. Brandt proclaimed:

> We will not allow ourselves to be poisoned by your madness. You believe yourselves to be part of a small but chosen elite whose destiny is to liberate the masses. You are wrong. The masses are against you.[23]

This basic distinction between violence arising organically from within exploited groups and violence initiated from the outside by terrorist factions not organically linked to the exploited social groups themselves is reflected in Sartre's attitude towards the revolutionary press.

VIOLENT WORDS AND VIOLENT ACTS

In March 1970, at the moment of publication of the eighteenth issue of the second series of *La Cause du Peuple*, the editor, Jean-Pierre Le Dantec, was arrested and charged with crimes against the state and incitement to theft, arson and murder. From this moment *La Cause du Peuple* was subject to regular seizures, so worried were the government authorities by the impact of its revolutionary propaganda. On 16 April, two days before the publication of the nineteenth issue of *La Cause du Peuple*, Le Dantec's successor, Michel Le Bris, was also arrested for the same reasons. It was at this point that Sartre intervened, accepting to become the editor initially of *La Cause du Peuple* and its supplements, and later of *La Cause du Peuple–J'Accuse*, as well as of numerous other revolutionary publications.[24]

Sartre's own individual contributions to the revolutionary press are, of course, difficult to assess, since to determine which articles or interviews bearing his name can legitimately be attributed to him is a highly problematical exercise. Given that the central strategy was to use Sartre as a shield to protect the revolutionary press from the arm of the law, much that bears his name is unlikely to have originated from Sartre himself. Even a cursory glance at the headlines of the second series of *La Cause du Peuple* is sufficient to reveal the deliberately provocative, potentially inflammatory and violent nature of the journalism itself:

> 'Bosses, it's time for war' (no. 11, August 1969)
> 'We are right to hold the bosses in confinement' (no. 13, October 1969)
> 'The blood of our brothers demands vengeance' (no. 15, January 1970)
> 'If you do not strike the boss, nothing will change' (no. 17, February 1970)
> 'Taking the bosses hostage is justice' (no. 33, January 1971)

The primary function of this style of journalism is neither to inform, nor to offer ideological instruction, but rather to encourage the readership to engage directly in a violent class war against the combined forces of international capital, the bourgeoisie, the government and the police. What is particularly striking in these articles is the highly dramatised picture that emerges of the social and political situation of France in the early 1970s. France is an occupied country controlled and administered by an oppressive élite of capitalist bosses in league not merely with the Gaullist government of the day, but also with all the opposition parties of the traditional left, including the PCF, willing to engage in servile collaboration. Alone, the courageous groups of Maoist freedom-fighters are waging a class war against the oppressors to liberate the French people from this capitalist tyranny.

It is perhaps too easy in retrospect to be dismissive of such far-fetched revolutionary scenarios. It needs to be borne in mind that the Pompidou government, particularly with Marcellin as interior minister, was undoubtedly perceived as particularly repressive, and that one or two quite brutal incidents involving the forces of law and order assumed a highly symbolic significance in the eyes of the extreme left. The aftermath of the death of Pierre Overney, for example, has already been discussed. Nonetheless, despite these caveats, the fact remains that the gulf between the social and political reality of France in the early 1970s and the manner in which it was reported in *La Cause du Peuple* was enormous. Sartre's attitude is described in the following terms by Simone de Beauvoir:

> [Sartre] let it be known that he did not accept all the ideas [of *La Cause du Peuple*]. In particular, he regretted that the GP compared its activities to those of the resistance, the role of the PC to that of collaborators, and that it spoke of an 'occupation' of France by the bourgeoisie and of the 'liberation' of French territory. These analogies seemed to him to be as ill-founded as they were ill-considered. But basically he got on well with the Maoists. He approved of their wish to revive revolutionary violence rather than

placing it in abeyance as the parties of the left and the trade unions were doing.[25]

Sartre is clearly unimpressed by what appears to him as a misguided and puerile attempt to make direct comparisons between the Nazi occupation of France between 1940 and 1944, and the social and political situation of France in the early 1970s. On the other hand, he unquestionably shared many of the revolutionary political views advocated by his Maoist comrades in the pages of *La Cause du Peuple*, in particular the highly disrespectful tone of verbal violence used to discredit political opponents. There is no doubting the fact that Sartre especially appreciated the Maoist willingness to show no respect whatsoever for the 'enemy', a readiness to engage in violent verbal conflict with the representatives of the established order. As he himself had remarked in 1964: 'I reproach myself for having been too respectful towards de Gaulle … I should have attacked him directly as a dangerous individual.'[26]

Given Sartre's antagonism to the 'resistance scenario', it is not surprising that his own contributions to both *La Cause du Peuple* and *La Cause du Peuple–J'Accuse* were focused specifically on the advocacy of the rights of ordinary people and on a frontal attack on the government and the class that supported it. His articles on the class basis of the French legal system, for example, reflect this approach.[27] Gradually, however, Sartre was forced to recognise the shortcomings of the revolutionary press.[28] Instead of seeking to explain the nature of government policy and consequently justify the need to struggle against it, *La Cause du Peuple* was indulging, Sartre argued, in facile and violent sloganising. Although generally in accord with the revolutionary politics of the Maoist groups of the period, he was nonetheless fully aware of the lamentable inadequacies of the press that articulated its political viewpoints. Sartre's growing disenchantment with the standard of news reporting in the revolutionary press, his rejection of ideological sloganising and of the uncritical and unmediated transposition of

Maoist ideas into a contemporary French context, his call for a broader basis of news reporting to include all potentially radical groups (the young, women, the petty-bourgeoisie), his ultimate rejection of sectarianism in favour of libertarianism, all this mirrored Sartre's views on Maoist revolutionary violence previously assessed. If revolutionary violence was to be both productive and moral, it would have to emerge organically from the needs of broad based communities. Similarly, effective revolutionary journalism must give expression to the multiple and varied voices of exploited communities, not the sectarian voice of a militant minority.

It is clear that throughout this revolutionary press interlude from 1970–4, there emerged a productive tension between Sartre's views and those of more sectarian Maoist militants, notably Benny Lévy, a tension that centres on the relationship between revolutionary violence and revolutionary news reporting. It is as if throughout this period there co-existed two competing discourses: at one level, a doctrinaire Maoist discourse in which pre-eminence was given to ideological instruction and violent, voluntarist sloganising; at another level, a more libertarian, Sartrean discourse in which pre-eminence was given to voicing the radical viewpoints of as wide a cross-section of an exploited community as possible. This secondary, libertarian discourse cannot, of course, be equated with liberalism. It is violently anti-authoritarian and aggressive in its tone, but it is not circumscribed by an ideological dogma that is completely alien to the social and political situation of France in the early 1970s. Sartre formulated this outlook in the following terms:

> For two years it has been a question of adapting Maoist strategy to the reality of France, not of transposing it word for word … The French Maoists speak readily of an ideological revolution: eliminating the fear of capitalism among the working-class population, notably through sequestrations, learning to resist, to hold out against

> repression, to overcome the respect that the ruling class instils in us. At the outset, I was in agreement with the Maoists on almost nothing at all; not against them, but at a distance from them. But they gradually demanded more than legal protection from me; I met them often and I became friends with them: gradually our thinking converged.[29]

The paradoxical conclusion that flows from the preceding analysis, therefore, is that Sartre was ultimately a stabilising influence in Maoist circles. This is not to say that he did not fully endorse the Maoist belief in the need to 'revive revolutionary violence through selective ... acts whose function was more or less symbolic'.[30] But it is to argue that what progressively became of paramount importance in Sartre's eyes as a political strategy was the effective use of the violence of words as ideological weapons to raise awareness of exploitation among different sections of a broad-based community. Sartre accordingly privileged the ideological violence of a genuinely popular revolutionary press as the most telling means of bringing about social change in post-1968 France; hence his commitment to the launch of *Libération* in April 1973. Such an interpretation does not reduce the status of Sartre's involvement in Maoist politics to a mere verbal gesture. Ideological consciousness-raising is a decisive element in the process of social transformation, and his understanding of a popular revolutionary press was aimed precisely at achieving this end. The fact that July, Lévy and Geismar parted company in 1974 with the more doctrinaire Maoist militants and chose to align themselves behind the broader-based platform of *Libération* is evidence of an undeniable evolution in Maoist politics between 1968 and 1974. By 1974 the violence of words had very definitely taken precedence over the violence of acts.

Part II
Sartre's Cultural Politics

6

Sartre and Commitment: Reinventing Cultural Forms

Throughout his life Sartre refused to envisage cultural activity from the perspective of passivity. Culture was neither a pre-established concept, nor a definitively finished art object. In true existential fashion, culture was always conceived as a process of continual invention and re-invention. Whether it was a question of artistic creativity, of critical interpretation or of public consumption, the overriding principle remained the need to call into question previous cultural theories and forms, previous cultural objects and icons, in order to subject them to the legitimate critical scrutiny of the contemporary world. The reason for this was not mindless antagonism to pre-established cultural norms, but rather the profound belief that the very essence of cultural activity was intrinsically heretical and critical; that in order to be true to its primary mission, cultural activity needed to be redefined by every new generation of artists and consumers of art. Not to engage in this process of redefinition and critical renewal would consign cultural activity to the status of a trivial formalism, and would lead ultimately to degeneration and the loss of dynamism in the processes of artistic creation and critical reception.

On 21 May 1968 in the *grand amphithéâtre* of the Sorbonne in Paris, Sartre outlined his ideas on cultural tradition and cultural revolution to a large and animated student audience:

> It is true that a cultural revolution needs to reflect on its cultural tradition. A cultural revolution presupposes a

> break with the present society within which previous cultural forms are exploited … So in one sense there is a break with tradition if you do not wish to become integrated in this society because the cultural traditions of this society are synonymous with the cultural forms of previous periods … However, although on the one hand a break with tradition is necessary, on the other it is impossible to negate completely those centuries of art or those cultural forms which have come before us. So you are obliged to negate these forms insofar as they are given to you, distributed to you within a bourgeois technocratic society, and at the same time you must salvage them in another way. In other words, *you have to reinvent tradition*. A cultural revolution cannot consequently be devoid of tradition, but must possess a tradition that it has shaped for itself. That is to say, you must envisage each work of art not as a lifeless given, but on the contrary as a minor revolution, a minor protest against previous cultural forms. (my italics)[1]

The key themes of Sartre's theory and practice of cultural commitment are articulated in this statement. Previous cultural traditions should neither be reverently worshipped nor barbarically destroyed. Previous cultural ideas and forms need on the contrary to be tested in the contemporary world. In essence, Sartre is describing a dialectical process of renewal in which the new is fashioned from the old with the tools of the present. Everything that Sartre wrote, whether it be philosophical, cultural or political, was ultimately framed within this dialectic of renewal. To some extent, the very breadth and range of Sartre's activities can be explained by this preoccupation with dialectical renewal. By extending his work across a variety of cultural forms, the scope for renewal was enhanced. From the fictional short story and novel forms to the theatre, from the film script to the critical essay, from biography and autobiography to journalism and militant political writings, from the philosophical treatise to radio and television broadcasts,

Sartre both challenged and was challenged by the issue of formal cultural renewal.

The second half of this book is therefore centred on three Sartrean experiments in the reinvention of cultural forms: the first highlights Sartre's exploration of satirical theatrical form, myth and politics (Chapter 7); the second assesses one example of Sartre's frequent experimentation with the critical essay form, focused in this instance on the work of Giacometti (Chapter 8); and the third examines Sartre's postwar encounter with the press and audiovisual broadcasting (Chapter 9).

DIVIDED CULTURAL ALLEGIANCES

I have already emphasised in Chapter 2 the importance of the notions of transition and division in Sartre's political itinerary. Transition and division are equally present in Sartre's cultural theory and practice. In the same way that Régis Debray interprets Sartre's political role as that of a 'ferryman' between the moralising attitudes of one generation of intellectuals and the progressively more committed stance of another,[2] so Roland Barthes envisages Sartre's cultural role from a similar divided and transitional perspective. Differentiating between a prewar phase during which 'great writers' such as Gide, Claudel, Valéry and Malraux exerted hegemonic cultural influence and power, and a postwar phase when traditional assumptions about the 'great writer' and the nature of cultural activity as a whole were being radically challenged, Barthes concludes that there is one person situated at the crossroads of these two cultures, located at the point of disintegration of the old and the birth of the new: 'there is one man who stands at the point of transition ... Sartre'.[3]

The relevance of Sartre's thoughts on cultural tradition articulated in the Sorbonne in 1968 to his own particular case are consequently strikingly and poignantly clear. Initiated into the formal practices of cultural activity during the 1920s and 1930s under the Third French Republic, Sartre was nonetheless most prolific and most celebrated as a writer and intellectual during the 1940s, 1950s, 1960s and 1970s under the Fourth and Fifth Republics when the previous cultural tradition was increasingly being called into question. Sartre's postwar cultural itinerary is consequently the record of a continual process of renegotiation in which the formal assumptions and criteria of one historical epoch are systematically tested against the value-system of another historical epoch in order, in Sartre's own words, to 'reinvent tradition'. The formal categories inherited from the cultural tradition of prewar Third Republic France are reassessed in the light of the cultural ambitions of the 'bourgeois technocratic society' of postwar Fourth and Fifth Republic France. The evolution of the theory and form of Sartre's cultural commitment is consequently illustrative of this process of renegotiation between two historical epochs.

Theory

Sartre's theory of commitment evolves significantly during the postwar period. Although there are inevitably shortcomings in any attempt to schematise a global theoretical evolution, it is not an excessively gross misrepresentation to highlight two key moments in this cultural evolution, themselves symptomatic of Sartre's general philosophical and ideological evolution from individualistic to more social preoccupations. Expressed simply, Sartre's notion of cultural commitment progresses from an activist phase in which the writer/artist is envisaged as capable of effecting significant social change, to a more reflective phase in which the writer/artist captures in his or her work the 'totality' of the social process.

The first 'activist' phase, which can be conveniently situated in the immediate postwar years, coincides with a moment of great optimism when cultural activity was considered to be at the epicentre of the social process, generating in its wake not only significant transformations in public awareness but also ultimately concrete social change itself. Based on the ideology of freedom, a work of art was defined in the Sartrean terminology of this immediate postwar period as the free appeal of the writer to the freedom of the reader. Writer and reader were entreated to enter freely into a pact based on trust and generosity. The notion of culture as an autonomous aesthetic object was consequently replaced by the idea of culture as a social process engaging writer/artist and 'reader' in a mutually rewarding activity whose focal point was the cultural text/object itself. The aesthetic object was consequently the site of a process of interaction between writer/artist and 'reader', the ultimate aim being revelation and disclosure of the world. It is in this sense that Sartre's early theory of commitment is both activist and militant, calling upon writers/artists, in theory at least, to commit themselves to the cause of freedom, and holding publicly accountable all those who failed to do so – hence the celebrated and now infamous phrase in 'Présentation des *Temps Modernes*' of 1945: 'I hold Flaubert and Goncourt responsible for the repression that followed the Commune because they did not write a single line to prevent it.'[4]

Such activist sentiments reflected above all else the ideological and social impulses of the immediate postwar period. In the aftermath of the defeat and occupation of the Second World War, the need for national reconstruction and regeneration was paramount. It is consequently not surprising that alongside political and economic reconstruction, an activist cultural regeneration began to take shape in which the emphasis was on a pronounced voluntarism which rapidly filled the vacuum left by oppressive and discredited right-wing ideologies. The extent to which Sartrean existentialism and the intellectual group centred on Sartre's influential review *Les Temps Modernes* shaped and influenced the process of postwar French ideological reconstruction cannot be underestimated.[5]

By the late 1950s and early 1960s, however, the discrepancy between the abstract voluntarism and activism of the early phase of Sartre's theory of cultural commitment and its practical impact in the world was becoming increasingly more evident. Far-reaching transformations not merely in the economic, social and political infrastructure of postwar France, but also, and equally significantly, in its cultural and technological superstructure, led to a fundamental reassessment of the role of the writer/artist. The linkage between culture and politics became greatly attenuated. Facile value-judgements of the political integrity of this or that writer/artist no longer predominated. Instead, there emerged a theory of cultural commitment centred on the idea of critical reflections of the total social process:

> We live surrounded by images. Literature offers us a critical image, a critical mirror of ourselves ... The real work of the committed writer is to display, to demonstrate, to demystify, to dissolve myths and fetishes in a bath of critical acid.[6]

Sartre consequently adjusted the radical and voluntarist theoretical pronouncements of the immediate postwar years to the transformed political, social and cultural environment of an increasingly technological and technocratic Fifth Republic France. This evolving theoretical stance is mirrored in Sartre's evolving exploration and exploitation of cultural forms.

Form

Sartre's 'reinvention of tradition' in the cultural sphere is perhaps most visible in terms of form. Unlike his close friend and contemporary, Paul Nizan, whose entire literary output was confined to the 1930s and consequently contained within the formal boundaries and expectations of a prewar historical situation, Sartre straddled the prewar and the postwar periods, thereby devising a more complex cultural response to the postwar period.

The formal manifestations of Sartre's cultural output mirror this divided or fractured historical situation in a quite uncanny fashion. Setting aside philosophical works, Sartre's writing project may be conveniently divided into four main areas: theatre, novel, biography/autobiography, and that series of texts which Sartre refers to as *'articles agissants'* (militant articles),[7] the essentially political writings of the ten volumes of *Situations* produced between 1938 and 1975, *Entretiens sur la politique* published in 1949 and *On a raison de se révolter* published in 1975.

Sartre's activity as a dramatist spans the period 1940 to 1965; as a novelist the period 1931 to 1949; as a biographer the period 1944 to 1972; as a 'militant' writer the period 1938 to 1980. The periodisation is itself illuminating, since it demonstrates an initial impetus in the sphere of the theatre and the novel, and a progressive shift of emphasis towards biography and 'militant' writings later in his life. In other words, there is a definite trend away from the more traditional literary forms towards experimentation with new forms such as 'existential biography' (including the critical essay) and militant and politicised writings, not to mention Sartre's forays into the spheres of radio and television broadcasting.

It is in this sense that Sartre 'reinvents a tradition', since his approach to form is one of exploration, interrogation, adaptation and renewal. That said, there are certainly differences of emphasis depending on the form in question. The integrity of conventional theatrical form is probably not seriously undermined in Sartre's cultural repertoire. The frequently subversive nature of the content of Sartre's plays often stands in contrast to the relative conservatism of the form in which the content itself is expressed. The intriguing aspect of Sartre's play *Nekrassov,* the subject of Chapter 7, is consequently that it seriously engages with the whole debate regarding the formal means of injecting political commentary effectively into theatrical form.

Sartre's experimentation with the novel form, on the other hand, exemplifies precisely this process of retention, adaptation and renewal. Both *La Nausée* and *Le Sursis* are primary exemplifications of Sartre retaining a traditional form in order to recast, to reshape and to reinvent the form itself. This process of reshaping and reinventing is of course taken one step further by Sartre through the creation of an entirely new form. I have argued in detail elsewhere that 'existential biography' is a new hybrid form invented by Sartre aimed at synthesising critical methodology and imaginary insight at a historical moment when, in Sartre's view, neither the traditional novel nor the conventional biography/essay were on their own structurally capable of responding adequately to the complexities of contemporary life in postwar France.[8]

Sartre's engagement with the critical essay form, whether it be in the sphere of art criticism (such as his work on Giacometti) or in more politicised and militant writings, as well as his exploration of the forms of the written press and of the audiovisual media, bear witness overall to a protracted negotiation with the full range of contemporary forms of cultural expression. Sartre's contribution to the cultural regeneration and reconstruction of postwar France consequently needs to be understood as a product of his unique position at the crossroads of the prewar and the postwar.

PROGRESSIVE-REGRESSIVE CULTURAL POLITICS

The progressive-regressive nature of Sartre's postwar cultural itinerary mirrors the progressive-regressive development of his postwar politics. In order to gain a final overview of this progressive-regressive trajectory, it is instructive to situate Sartre's cultural output within defined historical contexts. It would appear to me that Sartre's work in the postwar period can be appropriately divided into three key phases:

(i) 1945–58
(ii) 1958–68
(iii) post-1968.

1945–58: Cold War Synthesis

Although Sartre established his reputation as a writer in the late 1930s with the publication of *La Nausée* (1938) and *Le Mur* (1939), the almost gargantuan scope and complexity of his cultural activities did not become apparent until after 1945. Even a cursory glance at Sartre's intellectual output between 1945 and 1958 reveals an almost unrivalled level of achievement across a very broad range of disciplines and forms: philosophical and literary essays, political and social analyses, novels, plays, biographies, autobiography, art criticism. The major texts speak for themselves: *L'Age de raison* (1945), *Le Sursis* (1945), *L'Existentialisme est un humanisme* (1946), *Réflexions sur la question juive* (1946), *Baudelaire* (1947), *Situations I* (1947), *Les Jeux sont faits* (1947), *Les Mains sales* (1948), *Situations II* (1948), *L'Engrenage* (1948), *Orphée Noir* (1948), *La Mort dans l'âme* (1949), *Situations III* (1949), 'Drôle d'amitié' (1949), 'La Dernière Chance' (1949), *Le Diable et le bon dieu* (1951), *Saint Genet, comédien et martyr* (1952), 'Les Communistes et la paix' (1952), *L'Affaire Henri Martin* (1953), *Kean* (1954), *Nekrassov* (1956), 'Le Fantôme de Staline' (1957).

Despite the fact that Sartre's two principal philosophical texts, *L'Etre et le néant* and *Critique de la raison dialectique*, marginally pre-date and post-date the period under review, the originality, versatility and sheer quantity of Sartre's writings during this period are quite unparalleled. The scope of the three published volumes of *Situations* alone is sufficient to underline the exceptional quality of Sartre's output at this time. Equally, it needs to be noted that surrounding these major texts published between 1945 and 1958 is a myriad of other texts, notably the first draft of Sartre's autobiography written in 1953–4.

Sartre's productivity is perhaps not surprising, given that the decade or so immediately following the Second World War was the high-water mark of his intellectual notoriety and celebrity status. During this period a Sartrean world view gained almost hegemonic power in postwar

France, eclipsing previously dominant ideological trends, significantly challenging in particular Marxist and communist cultural and political perspectives. What is frequently overlooked in this assertion of a postwar Sartrean cultural moment is the fact that it coincided historically almost precisely with both the life span of the French Fourth Republic and with the onset and development of the first phase of the Cold War.[9] The previous analysis in Chapter 4 of Sartre's relations with the PCF during the Nizan Affair of 1947 has highlighted the extent to which Sartre's robust ideological 'psychology' matched the spirit of the times.

What is perhaps surprising is that the increasingly polarised international political situation during this period, far from debilitating Sartre artistically, on the contrary, provided him with an opportune environment in which his fertile imagination flourished. The key to Sartre's postwar artistic project, it seems to me, is located in this productive tension between politics and culture. In the same way that Nizan's cultural productivity during the 1930s was intimately linked to the increasingly polarised international political situation, so Sartre's cultural output in the immediate aftermath of the Second World War and throughout the first phase of the Cold War was dynamically connected to the conflictual and frequently polarised nature of the domestic and international politics of the period. Given the centrality of literature and culture to the social process in Sartre's postwar theory of commitment, it could not have been otherwise. The driving force in Sartre's cultural activity was precisely the attempt to inject social and political concerns within the fabric of his own writing practice. The real originality of his work is consequently synonymous with this sustained dialectical tension between political ambitions and beliefs and cultural forms and achievement. Between 1946 and 1958 Sartre's almost extravagent success as a writer and intellectual can ultimately be traced back to this productive tension between politics and culture, an unresolved creative synthesis that left in its wake a stream of writings that collectively embodies the spirit of the time.

1958–68: Third World Militancy and Reflection

1958 was a moment of deep despondency and disillusionment for Sartre. The demise of the Fourth Republic, the establishment of the Fifth Republic and the return to power of General de Gaulle was for Sartre the end of an era. The explicit Presidentialism of the new Republican system not only stood in marked contrast to Sartre's deeply held belief in political accountability, but also appeared to sound the death knell of left-wing political ambitions in France. The *political* consequence of this development has already been noted in Chapters 2 and 3. Sartre withdrew from involvement in French domestic politics between 1958 and 1968, focusing his attention instead on more distant colonial struggles in Cuba and Vietnam.

The *cultural* consequences of de Gaulle's accession to power also need to be clarified, however. Given that by 1958, Sartre had abandoned the novel form and had virtually completed his work as a dramatist,[10] the focus of Sartre's writing activities in the decade following 1958 was existential biography/autobiography and the more critically reflective and politically militant work of *Situations*. Key works in this period were: *Les Séquestrés d'Altona* (1959), *Critique de la raison dialectique* (1960), *Avant-propos à Aden Arabie* (1960), *Préface: Les Damnés de la Terre de Frantz Fanon* (1961), *Les Mots* (1964), *Situations IV* (1964), *Situations V* (1964), *Situations VI* (1964), *Les Troyennes* (1965).

Leaving aside Sartre's final forays into the realm of the theatre and the ground-breaking but much neglected *Critique*, the works listed above appear to fall into two categories: on the one hand those that reflect on the origins of a literary/artistic vocation, on the other those that engage in a highly stylised and dramatic fashion with third world political issues.

In the first category, Sartre's autobiography, *Les Mots*, is no doubt the archetypal text. A sustained and stylistic critical account of his own literary origins, *Les Mots* is a quintessentially reflective text whose critical venom is ultimately attenuated by the sophistication and brio of its own narrative devices.[11]

In the second category, texts such as the *Avant-propos à Aden Arabie*, centred on Nizan's journey to colonial Arabia in the 1920s but written in Cuba in the aftermath of the revolution, and the preface to Fanon's *Les Damnés de la Terre*, exemplify Sartre's work at its most critically violent. The dramatic lyricism of these texts focused on third world revolutionary struggles, however, is ultimately not entirely convincing because it is not adequately grounded in a deep understanding of the revolutionary struggles being portrayed. The overall impression is of a literary violence uprooted from genuine personal political involvement, of a disconnection between the cataclysmic violence frequently evoked in the words of the text and the unstated rootlessness of the personal experience of the writer.

In all the texts that Sartre produced in the ten years following the accession to power of General de Gaulle, there is a growing sense that the links between politics and culture are less self-evident, that the inner politico-cultural dynamism of the early phase of commitment is beginning to lose its impetus and direction.

Post-1968: Political and Cultural Separation

The cultural processes set in motion during the decade after 1958 reached their logical conclusion in the period following the events of May 1968. Although the events themselves constituted a political liberation for Sartre, enabling him finally to liquidate his links with the PCF and at the same time to consign Gaullism (at least in his own eyes) to the dustbin of history, his cultural activity finally lost the inner tension that originated in the dialectical interplay between politics and culture. The key texts in this period were the gargantuan biography of Flaubert, *L'Idiot de la famille*, and the politically militant writings for *La Cause du Peuple*, *J'Accuse* and *Libération*.

Sartre wrote the final version of *L'Idiot de la famille* between 1968 and 1972 when his thinking on the role of the writer/intellectual was undergoing profound change. He consequently lived a fundamental contradiction at this time: on the one hand producing an élitist literary work that could not possibly appeal to a popular readership, on the other supporting populist demands for the overthrow of the cultural dictatorship of his own bourgeois class.[12] By 1972 Sartre could not escape the fact that there was a glaring discrepancy between his actions as a pro-Maoist activist on the one hand and as a traditional bourgeois writer on the other. The gulf between the author of *L'Idiot de la famille* and the editor of *La Cause du peuple* could not have been greater. Sartre's political and literary activities definitively parted company. His politics became more and more extreme, more and more widely publicised. His literature became totally depoliticised and increasingly private. Unlike the immediate postwar period when Sartre's objective was to find a space for literature in politics, after 1968 Sartre tacitly accepted that there was no justifiable political role for the traditional bourgeois writer. Politics and literature became two quite separate pursuits. The dynamic tension of the postwar period was lost and Sartre proceeded to indulge in two quite separate activities, extremist political activism and unrestricted imaginary escapism. The link between politics and culture had finally snapped.

The ensuing analysis in Chapters 7, 8 and 9 accordingly needs to be placed within the context of Sartre's overall postwar cultural trajectory from dialectical tension, to reflection, to separation.

7

Myth versus Satire: The Dramatised Politics of Sartre's *Nekrassov*

'The need for satire is greatest when the political situation is most difficult', noted Sartre in 1955[1] just prior to the first performance of *Nekrassov*, his openly satirical play directed against the French anti-communist press.[2] Sartre could have been under no illusions that his dramatic denunciation of the lies and deceptions disseminated by the right-wing press during the Cold War period would be well received. Press reaction was almost universally hostile. Only *L'Humanité* and *Les Lettres françaises* enthusiastically and uncritically endorsed Sartre's political thesis and theatrical production. The pro-communist bias of the play inevitably alienated the majority of non-communist French drama critics, and effectively ensured that *Nekrassov* was peremptorily dismissed and then conveniently forgotten.

The polarisation of critical response to *Nekrassov* needs to be registered at the outset, since it graphically highlights the extent to which Sartre's play touched a sensitive political nerve-point in the psyche of the French bourgeoisie in the mid-1950s. So sensitive, in fact, that *Le Figaro* considered it necessary to sound the alarm bells one month before the first performance of the play, conjuring up in the minds of its readership the spectre of 'a work inspired by pure "crypto" communism'.[3] The analogy to be drawn between *Le Figaro*'s presentation of the play *Nekrassov* and *Le Soir à Paris*'s presentation of *Nekrassov*'s 'revelations' about the Soviet Union in the play itself is sufficiently ironic to merit comment here. The main thrust of the attack by *Le Figaro* was aimed at labelling the play not only as mortally boring and theatrically stultifying, but also as so mentally simplistic and politically inaccurate as to be an insult to the spectator's intelligence.[4] The views expressed in *Le Figaro* were reiterated in the columns of *Le Monde*: 'To laugh at M. Jean-Paul Sartre's eight variety sketches ... one needs to be wildly committed to Marxism and have a ferocious antagonism towards its opponents'.[5] Sartre was accused in no uncertain terms of having produced 'a variety show for which even the least talented cabaret singer from Montmartre would hesitate to claim responsibility'.[6]

In contrast, the communist response was predictably enthusiastic, and was inevitably interpreted by opponents as opportunism, an example of shabby political collaboration with a writer whom only a few years earlier the PCF had publicly denounced.[7] *L'Humanité*'s support for the play was unequivocal: '*Nekrassov* makes decent people laugh, makes the riffraff pull faces, and gives everyone food for thought'.[8] As for *Les Lettres françaises*, the key issue was not the self-evident theatrical quality of *Nekrassov*, but rather its political ramifications: 'With *Nekrassov*, the issue at stake is whether a play in opposition to the government and its press can survive the initial political intrigue to which it is subjected'.[9]

There were one or two exceptions to this Cold War political slanging match. *Combat*, for example, was genuinely supportive, providing Sartre with the opportunity to explain his intentions,[10] and publishing short extracts of the text,[11] while at the same time retaining enough critical distance to print a review written by an opponent of the play who had been personally ridiculed in *Nekrassov* itself.[12] Curiously, the Catholic response was not quite as completely negative as might have been expected. *Témoignage chrétien*, for example, although quick to point up what it perceived as the satirical limitations of the play, conceded nonetheless that *Nekrassov* contained dramatic scenes of high quality.[13] On the whole, however, critical response was polarised into two opposing camps, and the defenders of the play were very much in the minority.

The most lucid criticism at the time, however, came from Roland Barthes. Barthes perceptively demystified the nature of the hostile critical reaction, exposing the hypocrisy of those critics whose dismissive and antagonistic comments on alleged dramatic inadequacies were merely the visible manifestations of a thinly veiled sense of outraged indignation provoked by the explicit and unpalatable political message of the play itself:

> *Nekrassov* would have been saved and praised if it had been an ambiguous play (referred to as 'complex'), an inoffensive play (referred to as 'objective'), an uncommitted play (referred to as 'literary'). Unfortunately, *Nekrassov* is a resolutely political play, with a political viewpoint that is not appreciated; this is why it is being rejected.[14]

The critical reception given to *Nekrassov* is instructive, however, not simply to the extent that it highlights the political and ideological dimension of criticism itself, but also insofar as it exemplifies the manner in which interpretations of a given play ceaselessly fluctuate in relation to the political and ideological context in which it is produced. Proof, if proof were necessary, of the purely conjunctural nature of the critical reactions to *Nekrassov* in 1955 is provided by an examination of the responses to the play at later historical moments and in different cultures.

The British reaction to the play in 1956 and 1957, for example, is enlightening in this respect. The majority of critics on this side of the Channel, puzzled by the hostility that had greeted the play in France, were favourably impressed both by the English production in 1956,[15] and by the English translation of the text published in 1957.[16] In a similar vein, French responses to subsequent productions of the play in 1968 and 1978 were far more positive. Press reaction to the play when it was produced in the aftermath of the highly charged events of May 1968 at a moment when, paradoxically, Sartre's own attitude to the PCF was extremely antagonistic,[17] ranged from the highly enthusiastic to the mildly critical.[18] Ten years later, on the eve of a general election of crucial importance to the French Left, critical comments in the press were almost universally positive.[19] Different historical periods quite clearly elicit different critical reactions.

Relativising critical responses to *Nekrassov* in this way is a necessary prelude to any form of dispassionate re-evaluation of the play itself. The critical hostility and neglect to which the most overtly political of Sartre's plays has been subjected, has led to a failure to come to terms with the originality of the play itself. *Nekrassov* is unique in Sartre's repertoire not simply because it provoked almost universal condemnation when it was first produced (and the extremism of this condemnation, as has been seen, constitutes a fascinating sociological problem of cultural reception), but also, and more importantly, because it represents both an explicit political challenge to those power structures within a Western democracy whereby information is controlled and disseminated, and an implicit technical challenge to the very premises according to which Sartre's theatrical productions are themselves otherwise regulated.

The object of the following analysis is therefore twofold:

1. to assess *Nekrassov* in the light of Sartre's own statements on the theory and practice of theatre in order to clarify the play's dramatic structure and to determine its technical effectiveness;
2. to examine the play's satirical implications in order to assess whether an explicit and historically dated political bias inevitably assigns a purely conjunctural status to *Nekrassov*, or whether wider political themes enable it to retain a contemporary value in the late 1990s.

MYTH VERSUS SATIRE

A convenient point of departure is to establish the importance of myth in Sartre's theatre as a mediating function between the audience and social reality. Although the majority of Sartre's plays are replete with political and social connotations, throughout there is an attempt to present the dramatic production itself as an experience in which social reality is decanted into a more generalised, mythical form appealing to as wide an audience as possible, irrespective of differences of background, education, profession and so on within the audience itself. Hence, the driving force in Sartrean drama is the attempt to reach out to the audience via socio-political myths. The consequence of this quest for the mythical is the need to keep actual political events and political personalities at a distance:

> I do not think that theatre can emerge directly from political events ... Theatre must take these issues and transpose them into a *mythical* form. In my opinion, the commitment of a dramatist does not consist simply in presenting political ideas. This can be done in public meetings and in newspapers, and through militancy and propaganda. A dramatist who takes on these functions is perhaps of interest to the reading public, but s/he will not have produceded a play. (my italics)[20]

Throughout Sartre's theatre, from the production of *Bariona* in 1940 to that of *Les Séquestrés d'Altona* in 1959 and *Les Troyennes* in 1965, there remained a continuous quest for a 'mythical' representation of human reality which constituted, in Sartre's eyes, the essence of a truly dramatic experience, a half-way house between the passivity of an audience escaping into and emotionally entrapped within the dramatic situation itself, and the activity of an audience distanced from and critically participating in the dramatic action.[21]

The originality of *Nekrassov* is that it represents a quite explicit attempt by Sartre to break with his own theatrical theory and practice: 'this play demonstrates my wish to confront social reality without myths'.[22] It is quite significant, in fact, that Sartre's political ambitions at this juncture necessitated a fundamental reappraisal of his theatrical technique. The political objectives (satire of the right-wing, anti-communist press; contribution to the peace process in a Cold War context)[23] inevitably entailed a far more provocative and explicit theatrical stance than previously. Sartre's formal solution was to create what he described as 'une farce-satire', a contemporary version of the theatrical tradition of Aristophanes.[24] Quite clearly Sartre's objective was to invent a new form which made possible the explicit intrusion of politics (satire) within theatre, while at the same time retaining the credibility of the theatrical production itself (farce).

This is yet another example of Sartre's transitional status as a writer in postwar France. Although he was committed at one level to a project as a bourgeois dramatist, his ideological development compelled him to re-think the formal nature of this project in the light of current political allegiances to the PCF. The result is a political dislocation of the conventions of bourgeois theatre.[25] Whether or not the injection of explicit political satire succeeds formally will be discussed in a moment. What is indisputably the case, and Sartre himself was the first to admit as much, is that there is a glaring contradiction between the political objectives of a play such as *Nekrassov*, and the social ethos and structure of the bourgeois theatrical establishment in which it is produced:

> There is an incompatability between the issues that I wish to deal with and the current theatre audiences in Paris. To produce such a play in these conditions is in fact profoundly paradoxical.[26]

The evident social impotence of a theatrical piece doomed to failure when produced within the institutional and class structure of the Parisian theatrical scene, however, should not blind us to the fact that, in all probability, Sartre's vitality as a writer originates in a ceaseless interrogation of the limits of the cultural forms of his own class. *Nekrassov* is of interest precisely because it is a classic example of this interrogation process in Sartre's theatrical writings.

Nekrassov is set in the year 1952, at the height of the Cold War, during a by-election campaign in Seine et Marne. The government candidate, Mme Bounoumi, standing on a platform of German rearmament, is being challenged by candidates from both the communist and radical parties. The radical party candidate, Perdrière, although hostile to communism, is equally opposed to the rearmament of Germany. Since Mme Bounoumi's electoral success depends upon gaining the 100 000 or so votes of the radical party's candidate, and since this can only be achieved if Perdrière steps down in favour of Mme Bounoumi, the dramatic action of the play centres on a government-inspired propaganda campaign aimed at convincing the radical party candidate that the communist threat is greater than the threat of a rearmed Germany.

The vehicle of the propaganda campaign is the right-wing newspaper, *Le Soir à Paris*, and the central protagonist is Georges de Valera, a celebrated con-artist. Valera convinces the editorial board of the newspaper that he is the Soviet minister of the Interior, *Nekrassov*, who has 'chosen freedom', defected to the West, and is eager to reveal the iniquities of the Soviet communist system in the columns of *Le Soir à Paris*. Based on the Kravchenko affair of the late 1940s and early 1950s, *Nekrassov* focuses on the farcical and serious implications of a Macarthyite press campaign aimed at instilling fear and dread of communism in the hearts and minds of the general public.

This rapid synopsis of the content of the play highlights immediately the fact that Sartre has created a dramatic situation which is potentially at one and the same time extremely serious and extremely amusing. The serious literally juxtaposes the farcical, and it is this juxtaposition which is of central relevance for the purposes of this analysis. With *Nekrassov* Sartre deliberately chose to displace the centre of gravity of his theatrical production away from a preoccupation with myth and to offer as an experimental alternative a dramatic piece sliding constantly between the serious and the farcical. To what extent does this revised theatrical approach succeed?

It is important initially to stress that *Nekrassov* is an extremely amusing play. Despite adverse right-wing criticism which persisted in denying the genuinely humorous dimension of *Nekrassov*, the play contains many totally farcical episodes which succeed not only in warming the audience to the play itself, but also at the same time in keeping the audience's critical faculties on the alert: to laugh at the words and actions of Valera/Nekrassov is to remain at a distance from excessive emotional involvement in his plight.

This farcical dimension traverses the entire play from the opening scene where Georges, a typically Sartrean monster of pride and self-will, is first encountered abusing two tramps for having the audacity to interfere in his personal affairs and rescue him from a suicide attempt, to the final scene where the editorial team of *Le Soir à Paris*, all wearing rosettes emblazoned with the inscription 'Futurs Fusillés', one wearing a paper hat, one blowing into a reed pipe, two with streamers draped on their dinner jackets, squabble amongst themselves in apportioning blame for being taken in by Valera/Nekrassov.

Farcical humour is both situational and verbal, and verges frequently on slapstick comedy: Georges's initial encounter with l'Inspecteur Goblet during which the 'genius' of the former is contrasted amusingly with the 'mediocrity' of the latter (Tableau I, scene III); Georges's initial encounter with Véronique (Tableau III, scene I) in which verbal humour centred on male–female stereotypes is juxtaposed with the visual comedy of Georges holding his hands in the air while Véronique wipes his nose; the final scene of the 'soirée dansante chez Mme. Bounoumi' (Tableau VI, scene XV) in which Demidoff, a Soviet defector, creates pandemonium by getting drunk, repeatedly toasting the 'bolchevik-bolchevik' party, and eventually overturning the buffet table, the entire episode culminating in Goblet firing gunshots at Georges as he escapes from the reception party in the nick of time.

The most memorable and sustained farcical image in the play, however, is that of 'la Liste des Futurs Fusillés', the list of names revealed by *Nekrassov* of all those people in positions of power who are to be shot in the event of a communist takeover in France. Inclusion on the list is naturally judged as a mark of distinction within the circles of *Le Soir à Paris*, omission as a great dishonour. Jules Palotin's fear and joy at his inclusion on the list, Mouton's disappointment and social disgrace at being omitted, constitute high moments of humour in the play (Tableau IV, scene IV). Likewise, 'le Bal des Futurs Fusillés', the scene that was cut from the original production, is of an equally amusing nature, including as it does a barely disguised and farcical presentation of several well-known public personalities.[27]

The humorous dimension of *Nekrassov*, however, poses a fundamental question regarding its political effectiveness. Humour is frequently a diversion from reality, a means of escaping temporarily from the dreary ordinariness of daily existence. Given that farce can often constitute no more than an emotional escape-valve for a theatre audience, in what way can it be argued that Sartre's *Nekrassov* reaches beyond this escapist function in order to foreground a specific ideological thesis?

This particular question brings us back conveniently to Sartre's description of the play as a 'satirical farce'. What Sartre is attempting to achieve in *Nekrassov* is a fusion between farce and satire, an amalgamation between the reassuring ethos of farce and the disquieting implications of satire. A fusion of this kind is evidently fraught with difficulties, and many of the criticisms levelled against the play tend unconsciously to centre on the problematical status of such a hybrid form.

Two types of criticism, in particular, highlight this problematical status. First, the assertion that *Nekrassov* is a play which is insufficiently malicious to make effective satire; in other words, the softening effect of farce within the play blunts its satirical cutting edge. Second, the assertion that the impressive dramatic qualities exhibited in the first half of the play degenerate in the second half into tendentious and predictable moralising; in other words, the hardening effect of satire in the second half of the play undermines its dramatic qualities.

In brief, Sartre stands accused of having produced a play which is neither sufficiently hard-hitting to make for good satire, nor sufficiently light-hearted to make for good farce. It is precisely the paradoxical status of *Nekrassov*, half farce, half satire, which lays it open to criticisms of this type, and yet which constitutes ultimately its originality and, arguably, its genuine dramatic potency. To appreciate the full impact of Sartre's 'satirical farce', it is consequently necessary to reveal the structural development of the play itself.

Although both farce and satire juxtapose one another, and indeed frequently merge one with another throughout the dramatic action, it is nonetheless the case that the play progressively becomes more explicitly satirical and politicised in the second half (Tableaux V–VIII) during which a shift of emphasis from the farcical to the satirical takes place. This qualitative change in tone and emphasis is clearly signalled in the opening scene of Tableau V, where Georges begins to appreciate the extent of his powerlessness to control the social effects of the anti-communist propaganda conspiracy. Georges's growing realisation of his own impotence is the visible manifestation of a deliberate technical ploy designed to break the conventional flow of the dramatic action, to point up its 'literariness', artificiality, and hence to force the audience to an awareness of the fact that anti-communist propaganda is a *real* problem, not merely a pretext for a dramatic experience that can be conveniently neutralised as simply 'theatre'.

This technical disruption relays to the audience the fact that the dramatic action has shifted gear, and that a movement from the imaginary to the real has occurred. 'Aesthetic contemplation is an induced dream, and the transition to the real is a genuine awakening', noted Sartre in 1940.[28] Unlike Sartre's early thesis on the imaginary, however, in which he maintained that an audience experienced theatre in an imaginary mode (*'l'attitude imageante'*) which was qualitatively different from an experience of social reality (*'l'attitude réalisante'*), here,[29] in the second half of *Nekrassov*, reality suddenly intrudes on the stage. The audience is no longer able to contain the social implications of the play within an imaginary mould.

The structural mechanics of the play are thus deceptively simplistic. Although, at a purely narrative level, the progression is the anecdotal story of a swindler swindled, the true nature of the development is to be located in the interactive process between the production on stage and its significance in the minds of the audience. More precisely, there is a movement from a reassuring collusion between bourgeois audience and production predicated on the theatrical premises of farce, towards a disruptive denunciation of the audience itself predicated on the political premises of satire.

Throughout the first half of the play (Tableaux I–IV), and despite innumerable satirical allusions and references, the dramatic action is circumscribed within certain conventional limits. The satirical implications are enclosed, embalmed within a farcical matrix which by definition distances the action from reality and prevents the audience from taking the satire seriously. It is satire 'in parenthesis', satire that is 'just good fun', satire that is posing as satire and consequently merely an extension of dramatic licence. Hence, however serious the topic might be, whether it is a matter of the rearmament of Germany, the latest developments on the Cold War front, the true nature of an anti-communist press propaganda campaign, all is ultimately defused and neutralised within a global theatrical ethos in which farce constitutes an all-embracing dramatic reassurance. As long as Georges remains a successful 'con-artist', the world depicted remains farcical and unreal, and therefore not to be taken seriously.

In the second half, however, the tone and style of the play gradually but irreversibly change. As Georges is progressively perceived as an impotent pawn in the vast conspiracy of capitalist power relations, the true reality of the social situation forces itself upon the audience, and the serious implications of the play thrust themselves to the fore with an urgency that can no longer be contained within dramatic conventions as mere theatre, as diversion, as simple escapist farce. In Part Two of the play satire predominates. The theatrical mould of Part One is shattered and, although the tone is never entirely malicious and bitter since farcical elements persist, the audience is driven to an uncomfortable realisation of the serious social implications of the dramatic situation being enacted before its eyes.

In brief, then, Sartre's one genuine excursion into an explicitly political theatre led him to create a dramatic piece which oscillates constantly between two poles: the reassuring humour of farce and the accusing bitterness of satire. This hybrid form of satirical farce ensnares the audience in the first half by playing up the farcical, unreal dimension of the action, in order the more effectively to denounce the audience by implication in the second half when the reassuring mantle of farce takes a back seat to satire. In this sense it is possible to speak of a movement from myth to politics within the play itself. *Nekrassov* is a unique play to the degree that it is the only occasion when Sartre explicitly moves towards a destruction of the mythical dimension of the theatre itself in order to denounce unambiguously the inequalities, injustices and class oppression of social reality.

INDIVIDUAL DECEPTION VERSUS COLLECTIVE MYSTIFICATION

The political implications of *Nekrassov* are unambiguous. Unlike Sartre's other politically-orientated plays such as *Les Mains sales* and especially *Les Séquestrés d'Altona*, where the ambiguity of the social repercussions of individual acts blurs the field of interpretation, with the result that political positions lose their clarity, *Nekrassov* makes an explicit statement on anti-communist press propaganda. The unequivocal political thesis of this play explains its dramatic impact in the minds of the audience of the time.

Despite the hypocritical coyness with which the majority of right-wing critics masked their political outrage beneath a purely artistic and technical dismissal of the play, their sense of political outrage was nonetheless still visible.

Thierry Maulnier, for example, ridiculed by Sartre in *Nekrassov* as an 'eminent thinker' whose anti-communist newspaper articles amounted to no more than excellent recruitment propaganda for the PCF (Tableau IV, scene I), was doubtless sufficiently incensed not only to deliver a blistering attack in 1955 on what he perceived as the inadequacies of the political thesis at the heart of the play,[30] but also to recall its political thesis one year later in an editorial entitled 'Nékroutchov?', amalgamating *Nekrassov* and Krushchev at the time of the latter's revelations on Stalin.[31]

Gabriel Marcel likewise considered it important to point out the potentially dangerous impact of the play:

> In the politically charged situation confronting France and the Western nations in June 1955, this play, were it to be taken seriously, can legitimately be judged to be dangerous ... since it tends towards classifying as hysterical publicity or mindless Macarthyism the very real anxieties that we might have regarding the future of the free world, we who know where we stand on the Polish, Hungarian or Czech paradise.[32]

In what way, then, does the political theme of *Nekrassov* force itself so imperiously on the audience? The answer resides both in the technical progression of the play previously discussed, and in a quite decisive shift of emphasis in the second half of the dramatic action from the theme of individual deception to that of collective mystification. Expressed more simply, whereas in the first half of the play the dominant theme is the life-style of an individual protagonist with whom the audience can to some extent identify despite his farcical unreality, in the second half the dominant theme is the all-encompassing power of the agencies of collective socialisation, in this instance the

Press Empire which reduces individuals to mere ciphers in a wider political scheme. In Part Two the importance of Georges de Valera to the dramatic action diminishes in direct proportion to his control over events. What emerges in the second half is the irresistible presence of a gigantic social institution, a huge machine feeding on the lives of ordinary men and women in order to construct a social fantasy by means of which to control public opinion. 'Institutions and structures determine men ... This is why a left-wing satire must be a satire of institutions and not of men', noted Sartre at the time.[33]

Although Sartre himself was subsequently to assert in a typically self-critical vein that the play was to some extent flawed since it was excessively centred on the con-artist rather than on the newspaper,[34] it is nonetheless my contention that this play achieves a successful balance between individual and collective experiences. By implicating the audience directly in the life-style of an individual (Tableaux I–IV), in order the more effectively to highlight (Tableaux V–VIII) the enormity of the social institution which manipulates people's lives, whether they be surreal con-artists like Georges de Valera or ordinary readers of daily newspapers, Sartre created with *Nekrassov* a genuine left-wing satire of a right-wing press institution.

The impotent status of Georges at the end of the dramatic action:

> 'Manipulated! manipulated like a child! Over there I was an instrument of hatred; here I am an instrument of history!' (Tableau VII, Scene I)

is a mirror-image of the impotent status of the audience, and by extension of daily newspaper readers whose minds are ceaselessly manipulated by a powerful press machine. It is doubtless significant that Georges is absent from the final scene of the play, which is devoted to the activities of the editorial board of the newspaper. Georges's absence from the set merely underlines the dominant theme of

Nekrassov; that the social swamps the individual, that the individual powers of deception of one man are no match for the collective powers of public mystification of a huge Press Empire. Beyond the lightweight banter and repartee of Georges de Valera, what remains in the minds of the audience at the end of *Nekrassov* is an awareness of the awe-inspiring power of the press to manipulate the minds of ordinary people.

The production of *Nekrassov* in 1955 undoubtedly marked a turning-point in Sartre's relations with the media. Sartre's quite explicit attack on Pierre Lazareff's Press Empire has even been interpreted in some quarters as the first stage in the struggle for power and prestige between intellectuals and media tycoons in postwar France which was to culminate in the 'charismatic fall of intellectuals'.[35] Whatever the value of this wider social thesis, it remains indisputably the case that *Nekrassov* constitutes a paradoxically emblematic example of Sartre's cultural originality and social powerlessness. At one level the play demonstrates a highly original reworking of a conventional cultural form; at another, it illustrates the social impotence of such forms when compared to the power exerted by the press, radio and television. As Sartre himself was forced to admit:

> The balance of power between a newspaper such as *Le Figaro*, for example, with a daily readership of four or five hundred thousand, and the one hundred thousand or so spectators of a very successful play, is evidently weighted towards the newspaper.[36]

In 1961 Sartre argued that it was not the dramatist's vocation to usurp the political function of the press.[37] Paradoxically, with *Nekrassov*, he had already succeeded at a technical and thematic level in usurping this political function, only to remain aware that in terms of social impact a theatrical production can never rival a newspaper. In postwar France the press, radio, and most importantly nowadays television, are the prime agents of information, opinion-forming and cultural production and socialisation.

Throughout the postwar period the technological dimension of the media has been revolutionised, enhancing in the process the strength of their political and social impact. The continuing relevance of the political thesis at the heart of *Nekrassov* could consequently not be more starkly exemplified. Beyond the historical and ideological limitations of its original moment of production during the Cold War period, beyond the sociological contradiction of the enactment of an anti-establishment play within an establishment institution, beyond the cultural contradiction of a traditional theatrical form contesting the very premises on which new mass audience and technologically-orientated media forms are predicated, *Nekrassov* retains a dramatic potency and biting satirical edge today. At a moment when we are witnessing the technological explosion of the new media, Sartre's *Nekrassov* offers a striking mirror-image of the manner in which the media empire presents information and manipulates public opinion.

8

Ideological Art Criticism: Sartre and Giacometti

The 1993 exhibition at the Tate Gallery, 'Paris Post War: Art and Existentialism 1945–55', focused attention on eleven artists working in the French capital in the aftermath of the Liberation.[1] The primary thrust of the exhibition was accordingly to place the sculpture and painting of Giacometti, Dubuffet, Picasso, Richier, Hélion, Gruber, Van Velde, Michaux, Fautrier, Artaud and Wols within the effervescent ideological and artistic context of the time. Given that Alberto Giacometti was perceived by many to be 'the central figure of the exhibition',[2] the aim of the following analysis is to explore the links between Giacometti, existentialism and Sartre using the Paris Post War exhibition as a convenient point of entry into the debate.

The argument that follows will be organised in four parts. First, I shall discuss a series of preliminary issues in order to situate Sartre's work on Giacometti in relation to the 1993 exhibition. This will provide a useful contextualisation of the debate surrounding Sartre's critical evaluation of Giacometti's work. Second, I shall assess the fundamental premises, both methodological and ideological, underlying Sartre's attitude towards the visual arts in order to clarify the nature of Sartre's intentions when speaking of painters and sculptors. Third, I shall concentrate specifically on Sartre's relations with Giacometti, both biographical and textual, and will evaluate the two major critical essays that Sartre devoted to Giacometti, the first in 1948 on Giacometti's sculpture,[3] the second in 1954 on Giacometti's painting.[4] Finally, I shall offer one or two concluding thoughts on the Sartre–Giacometti relationship.

INITIAL CONSIDERATIONS

It is instructive initially to focus on Sartre's relationship to the 1993 exhibition. What was particularly striking in the exhibition was not solely the visual impact of the paintings and sculptures on view, but also what might be aptly referred to as the 'invisible ideological accompaniment' to the exhibition – that is to say, the contextualising ideology of existentialism, and the contextualising intellectual presence of Sartre himself. Of the eleven artists in the exhibition, Sartre wrote significant critical essays on Giacometti and Wols,[5] discussed tangentially the work of Picasso[6] and Artaud,[7] and was of course the most prominent intellectual figure linked to existentialism. The fascinating array of documents of the period displayed in the exhibition offered a vivid illustration not only of the contextualising weight of existentialism as an ideological backdrop to the paintings and sculptures, but also of the contextualising intellectual presence of Sartre himself.

And yet, despite what would appear to be a productive interaction between the formal shape and texture of art objects and the ideological and cultural context in which these art objects were produced, there nonetheless remains an unwillingness in certain quarters to acknowledge either the impact of existentialist ideology on the artistic production of the time, or the legitimacy of Sartre's existential critique of given painters and sculptors. In essence, therefore, the following analysis of Sartre and Giacometti constitutes an exploration of the manner in which formal art objects co-exist with ideology and history. Expressed more simply, the fundamental question that I am asking is at one level the extent to which existentialism was genuinely reflected and refracted in the art objects displayed in the exhibition, and at another level the extent to which Sartre as a philosopher and a literary intellectual can legitimately speak in an authoritative manner about painting and sculpture.

At the one-day conference linked to the exhibition,[8] there emerged a litany of criticism directed specifically against what was doubtless perceived as the oppressive and restrictive ideological sway of Sartre and existentialism over the production and interpretation of the painting and sculpture of the postwar period. Did the ideology of existentialism really contribute anything at all to the artistic practice of the time? Do Sartre's critical essays on Giacometti and Wols ultimately reveal anything other than Sartre's own ideological idiosyncracies? A few examples from the conference are instructive in this respect.

The artists in the exhibition, it was argued, owe far more to surrealism than to existentialism; Sartre's eagerness to assassinate a literary surrealism in *Qu'est-ce que la littérature?* has as its counterpart a deliberate silence on Sartre's part when speaking of the early work of Giacometti, for example, itself heavily influenced by surrealism;[9] Sartre's physical sight was defective, with the consequence, so it was alleged, that his critical appreciation of the visual arts was accordingly impaired and by implication invalid;[10] Sartre's theoretical critical interpretations bear very little resemblance to the artistic practice of painters and sculptors such as Giacometti;[11] Merleau-Ponty's artistic vision, described variously as 'a descent to the unifying roots of phenomena' and as the attempt to apprehend 'the carnal essences of things' was judged to coincide more precisely than Sartre's critical views with Giacometti's artistic practice;[12] Artists were in general more sympathetic to Camus than to Sartre since

> Sartre was an intellectual terrorist; his ideas reflect his own preoccupations and say more about himself than about the artist under discussion.[13]

This last statement by Olivier Todd concludes my preliminary comments and leads conveniently into the second part of my analysis, centred on the fundamental premises underlying Sartre's attitude towards the visual arts.

SARTRE – INTELLECTUAL TERRORIST

Todd's statement is a useful starting-point, since in my opinion he is at one level absolutely right: Sartre was an intellectual terrorist. Yet he is at another level fundamentally wrong: Sartre's interpretations are not invalidated because predicated on intellectual terrorism. It is this particular paradox that I would like to explore further in what follows.

Sartre's terroristic attitude to his intellectual peers is well documented. As has already been highlighted in Chapter 4, Jean Cau, his personal secretary from 1946 until 1957, considered that there was in Sartre's character 'a form of intellectual imperialism and totalitarianism'.[14] This intellectual terrorism, this readiness to excommunicate others, was doubtless most graphically highlighted in the Sartre–Camus polemical dispute in 1952.[15] There were in fact many other examples of Sartre's terroristic attitude to his intellectual peers; his polemical assaults on Aragon,[16] Mauriac,[17] Aron[18] are but three illustrations of this excommunicatory attitude.

In many ways, Sartre's temperamental outlook merely coincided with the cultural and ideological climate of the time. In a postwar period when previous ideologies were perceived as bankrupt, existentialism filled the intellectual vacuum that had appeared by publicly denouncing and denigrating its competitors. Sartre's attack on surrealism and the violent polemic between the existentialist group and the French Communist Party in the immediate postwar period can largely be explained as the conflictual process whereby the new ideology of existentialism established itself as the hegemonic cultural reference system of the time. Sartre was merely the most visible and widely publicised exponent of this intellectual process.[19] And it needs to be emphasised, in particular, that Sartre's essays on Giacometti were produced in 1948 and 1954 at a time of increasingly polarised Cold War ideological conflict when intellectual confrontation was intense.

The critical process that Olivier Todd dismisses as 'intellectual terrorism' is in fact remarkably similar to what Roland Barthes designates as 'ideological criticism'.[20] The aim of the ideological critic is not principally to offer an explanation of the original work either in its own terms of reference or via the lens of cliché-ridden liberal critical conventions, but rather to confront and to interrogate the work in question with a contemporary ideological language.[21] Sartre's art criticism needs to be viewed in this light: it is highly original, but it is also explicitly ideologically motivated. Its aim is to test the intristic qualities of painting or sculpture against certain existential assumptions, both formal and social, in order to release new interpretations of the work itself. Although Sartre himself would doubtless have argued for the pre-eminence of his particular ideological interpretation over all others, it would naturally be as misguided to accept Sartre's interpretations uncritically as it would be to reject them out of hand. My contention is that this process of ideological interpretation does indeed offer new insights, does force us to review our conventional codes of interpretation. It is not the total picture. It is a very specialised, frequently idiosyncratic point of view, but it is far from being irrelevant and devoid of interest as Sartre's critics might contend.

It is, of course, important to draw attention to two other purely circumstantial aspects of Sartre's ideological criticism of artists in postwar Paris. The first is the increased publicity and hence visibility given to the works of Giacometti and Wols, for example, through mere association with the notorious name of Sartre. The existential cachet given to their work in Sartre's articles undoubtedly gave them greater prominence in the public domain. At the same time, and this is the second point, as Olivier Todd noted during the Tate conference, Sartre did not write extensively on these artists. In other words, they were not analysed in such depth and detail as to be subsequently rendered virtually creatively impotent through excessive personal exposure, as was allegedly the case with Jean Genet in the wake of the publication of Sartre's totalising biography, *Saint Genet, comédien et martyr*.[22]

Although it would be an overstatement to maintain that Sartre's ideologically motivated art criticism constitutes a coherent methodological system,[23] it is nonetheless the case that there are recurring value-judgements and assumptions in Sartre's critical assessments that need to be clarified before directing attention specifically at Giacometti. Perhaps the most important point to stress is Sartre's refusal to separate the work of art from the life of the artist; a commitment, in other words, to interpret painting and sculpture as an intentional artistic project, not as a collection of formal art objects. In an interview with Michel Sicard towards the end of his life,[24] Sartre emphasised the importance of understanding the link between individual artists and the work that they produced. Art is not in Sartre's eyes a finished product, but rather a creative process. A Sartrean interpretation of a painting or a sculpture therefore necessitates revealing the artistic project at the basis of the work itself, an artistic project that has its roots in human freedom. This recurring quest for an intentional artistic project is ultimately predicated on two assumptions, one political, the other philosophical. It is instructive to examine these briefly before assessing Sartre's account of Giacometti.

At a political level, Sartre stands resolutely opposed to artists who allow themselves to be used by governing élites to perpetuate the status quo, to depict society as serene and unproblematical, thereby justifying the rights and privileges of the ruling class. The celebrated passage in Sartre's novel, *La Nausée*, in which the principal character Roquentin visits Bouville Museum in order to view portraits of the town's ruling élite, is highly instructive in this respect:

> All who belonged to the Bouville élite between 1875 and 1910 were there, men and women, meticulously depicted by Renaudas and Bordurin …
>
> They had been painted with great care; and yet, under the brush, their features had been stripped of the

> mysterious weakness of men's faces. Their faces, even the feeblest, were as clear-cut as porcelain: I looked at them in vain for some link with trees or animals, with the thoughts of the earth or water. The need for this had obviously not been felt during their lifetime. But, on the point of passing on to posterity, they had entrusted their faces to the dredging, drilling, and irrigation by which, all around Bouville, they had transformed the sea and the fields. Thus, with the help of Renaudas and Bordurin, they had enslaved the whole of Nature: outside themselves and in themselves. What these dark canvases offered to my gaze was man re-thought by man, with, as his sole adornment, man's finest conquest: the bouquet of the Rights of Man and Citizen ... The power of art is truly admirable ...
>
> I had walked the whole length of the Bordurin–Renaudas Room. I turned round. Farewell, you beautiful lilies, elegant in your little painted sanctuaries, farewell, you beautiful lilies, our pride and *raison d'être*, farewell, you Bastards.[25]

Sartre's art criticism is suffused with an implicit negative value-judgement against all artists who allow their work to be used to promote the political ends of those in positions of power and influence. The most striking example of this anti-establishment view of art is doubtless Sartre's rejection of Titian in favour of Tintoretto. Whereas Titian's artistic virtuosity was in Sartre's opinion exploited to smooth over the rough edges of existence and to present in his paintings a beautiful but false image of an eternal, divinely ordered Venice which was reassuring to the establishment, Tintoretto's genius on the contrary lay in using his skill as a painter to dismay this same establishment by highlighting in his paintings the human pain, anguish and suffering of sixteenth-century Venetian life. Tintoretto's paintings, Sartre maintains, are an act of profanation against divine order. His tenacious and systematic exploitation of three-dimensional perspective destroys the pictorial illusion of a divinely ordered world. In Tintoretto's paintings God is literally brought down to earth. The divine assumes mortal proportions. This terrifying discovery is, according to Sartre, masked in the paintings of Titian. Tintoretto's skilful exploitation of perspective is such as to draw us totally into the depths of the painted canvas, into the yawning chasm of existence that has opened up between the divine and the human world.[26]

The example of Tintoretto is appropriate, since it leads naturally to the second assumption underpinning Sartre's art criticism. In this case, the issue at stake is philosophical, or to be more precise phenomenological, rather than political. Sartre is attracted to Tintoretto to the degree that he portrays the movement of human existence rather than the stasis of a divine order. Sartre's preference for art which depicts the mobility of consciousness as opposed to the inertia of being is prefigured in the early phenomenological essay, 'Visages',[27] for which it should be noted Wols produced four dry-point engravings for the 1948 Seghers reprint of the original text.[28] Sartre offers the following phenomenological description of the face:

> One discovers among things certain beings that are called faces. But they do not exist as things. Things do not have a future and the future surrounds a face like a mantle… Things are heaped up in the present, they shiver in their place without moving; a face throws itself forward from itself in space and time. If the capacity of the human mind to go beyond itself, and to go beyond all things, to escape from itself and lose itself outside itself… is called transcendence, then the meaning of a face is *visible* transcendence.[29]

The opposition that Sartre posits here between the inert solidity of being and the explosive mobility of consciousness translates itself in artistic terms into a rejection of painting and sculpture which reduce the human form and the human experience to statuesque immobility. 'Statues', notes Sartre, 'are bodies without a face; blind, deaf bodies with neither fear nor anger.'[30] The success of a work of art in Sartre's eyes resides therefore in its capacity to go beyond the statuesque and create the impression of what he refers to as '*visible* transcendence'.

In a revealing anecdote in his autobiography, *Les Mots*, Sartre discusses an aptitude test that he underwent in 1948 at Utrecht. The test itself consisted in selecting an image which created in the eyes of the onlooker the greatest impression of speed. Sartre selected the image of a motor boat springing forward. He rationalised his choice in the following terms:

> The reason for my choice came to me immediately: when I was ten I had the impression that my prow was cleaving the present and wrenching me away from it; since which time I have been running, am still running. Speed is conveyed, to my eyes, less by the distance covered in a specific lapse of time than by its wrenching power.[31]

Sartre wrenching himself from the present, running towards the future in search of himself: a striking image which has profound implications for his art criticism. Sartre is fascinated by works of art which convey the notion of movement, of wrenching from the present and of headlong flight towards the future, in short, of visible transcendence.

SARTRE AND GIACOMETTI

It is interesting at the outset to explore the nature of Sartre's relations with Giacometti from a biographical perspective, that is to say, by assessing the manner in which their relationship is presented initially in Simone de Beauvoir's *La Force de l'âge*, published in 1960, secondly in Sartre's autobiography, *Les Mots*, published in 1964, and finally in de Beauvoir's *Tout compte fait*, published in 1972. Such an exploration is appropriate to the extent that it rejoins the theme of intellectual terrorism evoked earlier. These three texts were produced by two prominent postwar French intellectuals whose ideological beliefs and values were virtually identical, and one of whose principal aims was to impose a shared vision of their common history in their memoirs and autobiographical writings. In many ways the Sartre–de Beauvoir writing duo constitutes the reign of double terror, each one of them complementing and confirming the ideas of the other. A close reading of the relevant sections of these three texts demonstrates a certain ricochet effect between them and a sustained attempt to present an existentialist image of Giacometti the artist.

In *La Force de l'âge*, de Beauvoir highlights three main aspects of Giacometti's artistic endeavour. First, she stresses what she perceives as Giacometti's appetite and curiosity for life, linking this character trait to a car accident in which Giacometti had been involved, and which had prompted him to reflect on death. 'Even death was in his eyes a living experience', notes de Beauvoir.[32] Second, she underlines the similarity of artistic temperament between Sartre and Giacometti: 'there existed between Sartre and Giacometti', she alleges, 'a deep affinity: they had wagered everything, one on literature, the other on art, and it was impossible to decide which one of them was the most fanatical'.[33] Third, she is at pains to detach Giacometti from his surrealist past, which is presented as a misguided artistic avenue:

> He had formerly been linked with the surrealists … but for two or three years this path had appeared to him as a dead-end. He wanted to return to what he now judged to be the true problem in sculpture: recreating the human face … Giacometti's viewpoint linked up with that of phenomenology … the influence of the surrealists had led him, like so many others, to confuse the real world with the imaginary.[34]

Hence, in the space of a few pages de Beauvoir offers a picture of Giacometti as an exemplary existential artist-hero: passionate about life to the point of death, committed as fanatically to sculpture and painting as Sartre was to literature, and repentant of his dubious surrealist past to the point that he is entirely incorporated into a revised phenomenological reference system.

Sartre continues this process of incorporation of Giacometti within an existentialist framework in his autobiography, refining and developing the anecdote concerning the motor accident:

> More than twenty years ago, one evening as he was crossing the Place d'Italie, Giacometti was knocked down by a car. Injured, his leg twisted, he was at first aware, in the lucid faint into which he fell, of a kind of joy: 'At last something's happening to me!' I appreciate his radical attitude: he expected the worst; this life which he loved to the point of never wanting any other had been upset, perhaps smashed by the stupid violence of chance. 'So', he thought, 'I wasn't born to be a sculptor or even to live; I was born for nothing'. What excited him was the menacing order of causes suddenly unmasked and imposing on the lights of the city, on man, on his own body, flattened in the mud, the paralysing aspect of a disaster: to a sculptor, the kingdom of the mineral world is never far off. I admire this will to welcome everything. If you like surprises, you must like them to this extreme, even to those rare lightning-flashes which reveal to its lovers that the earth was not created for them.[35]

It is clear from the context from which this extract is taken that Sartre is highlighting Giacometti's allegedly radical attitude to the contingency of existence in order to make an effective contrast with what he perceives as his own counterfeit radicalism as a child: 'my adversities', he notes, 'would never be anything but tests or the means of writing a book'.[36] The important point for the purposes of this analysis, however, is that Sartre retains in his autobiography the image of Giacometti the radical existential artist-hero.

Eight years later, a slightly discordant version of events emerges in a subsequent volume of de Beauvoir's memoirs, *Tout compte fait*. De Beauvoir reveals Giacometti's animosity towards Sartre for the latter's account of the car accident in *Les Mots*. The truth, according to Giacometti, was that he had been about to depart for Zurich, leaving behind a woman that he loved. When, he alleges, he had been knocked down by a car in the Place des Pyramides (not the Place d'Italie), he had been delighted because the accident had enabled him to remain in Paris with the woman in question. According to Giacometti, the purely personal and emotional reasons underlying his reaction to the accident had been transformed by Sartre into an affair of metaphysical significance. According to Sartre and Simone de Beauvoir, on the other hand, such a mundane event would not have attracted their attention unless Giacometti himself had endowed it with such a significance. 'The discrepancy between the two versions undoubtedly originated with him, and we never managed to understand it', concludes de Beauvoir.[37]

This brief analysis of extracts from three texts illustrates two principal points: first, the writings of de Beauvoir and Sartre function as complementary and corroborating devices for presenting an image of Giacometti as a radical existential hero who had come to realise the error of his surrealist past, and who had wagered his very existence on an artistic project framed within an existential/phenomenological perspective; second, this ideological interpretation of Giacometti's artistic enterprise, however original and insightful it might be in its own right, frequently stands in contradiction to the lived experience of the artist himself. Giacometti's resentment at Sartre's account in *Les Mots* of the significance of his car accident doubtless reflects on a minor scale Genet's dizzying experience when discovering Sartre's version of his life and work in *Saint Genet, comédien et martyr*. All this needs to be borne in mind when scrutinising Sartre's two seminal essays on Giacometti's sculpture and painting.

IDEOLOGICAL ART CRITICISM

'La Recherche de l'Absolu', published for the first time in *Les Temps Modernes* in January 1948, is a classic example of ideological criticism. It constitutes an existential reading of Giacometti's sculpture, a sustained interrogation of Giacometti's artistic project through the critical lens of existentialism. Sartre's critical interpretation begins with a reference to what he refers to as Giacometti's 'antediluvian' expression. At the Tate conference Olivier Todd objected to this description, arguing that Giacometti's face was remarkably expressive, that he was not entirely sure what an 'antediluvian' face actually looked like, and that in any case it had little, if anything, to do with Giacometti's sculpture. What needs to be emphasised, however, is that Sartre is strategically placing Giacometti within the existential/phenomenological reference system already outlined. Since, in Sartre's view, all previous sculptors have merely produced lifeless bodies, petrified effigies of man and woman cast in stone, Giacometti's artistic enterprise must be placed in a temporal perspective that pre-dates even the earliest classical sculptors. It is not sufficient simply to disengage Giacometti from his surrealistic origins (a task previously undertaken by Simone de Beauvoir in her memoirs); it is necessary rather to situate Giacometti at the very origins of the sculptural enterprise itself. 'After three thousand years', notes Sartre, 'Giacometti's task ... is to prove that sculpture is possible ... there is just one problem to be resolved: how to make a man from stone without petrifying him?'[38] Sartre's description of Giacometti's face as 'antediluvian' is therefore a strategic sign to the extent that it conveys the idea that Giacometti's artistic project is located at the very origins and roots of sculpture itself. By situating Giacometti's artistic enterprise before and outside all classical models, Giacometti the sculptor implicitly assumes the status of an archetypal existential hero. He is absolutely free, since he is not dependent on prior cultural influences; his existential project is a ceaseless daily struggle with raw materials in an effort to sculpt a living existence from inert matter. The term 'antediluvian' is accordingly highly significant for Sartre's overarching thesis.

Giacometti is presented as an artist generally dissatisfied with the labours of his work, insofar as his activity as a scuptor is likened to the ceaseless production of rough drafts and sketches, ultimately aborted and destroyed because failing to coincide with the ideal that he is seeking to attain. There is an implicit admiration in Sartre's account for Giacometti's reluctance to preserve his finished sculptures. Their existence in bronze or photographic form is explained, for example, in purely financial terms. Giacometti's decision to exhibit his works for the first time in fifteen years is interpreted solely as the need to keep body and soul together. It is as if the sculptor's overriding objective in Sartre's eyes is to create weightless plaster figures situated half-way between being and nothingness, and destined to exist for a few hours only: 'Never was matter less eternal, more fragile, closer to being human', notes Sartre.[39] The destruction of these ductile, perishable plaster forms becomes symbolic in Sartre's eyes of the paradox of Giacometti's enterprise, since only the elimination of the sculptural residue of his work prevents the almost inevitable return to the lifeless being of inert matter.

And yet, in the end, it is Sartre's contention that Giacometti locates a technical solution to the inertia of classical sculptural form. The ideal, in Sartre's eyes, is to create sculpture which captures the movement and the indivisible unity of human existence. In other words, sculpture must create the illusion that the form portrayed is not a collection of parts, not a juxtaposition of techniques, but a synthetic, unified movement. Drawing on the fundamental distinction that he had previously established in *L'Imaginaire* between the manner in which consciousness apprehends the real and the imaginary, Sartre contends that in the past sculptors had confused imaginary space with real space.[40] They did not sculpt what they actually saw of the human figure from a given viewpoint, but rather introduced into the imaginary space of the sculpture details that they had acquired from the real world, from their prior knowledge of human anatomy, for example. Unlike the painter, whose creation in a two-dimensional space did not lead to a confusion between the real and the imaginary (the painting is a two-dimensional artefact portraying a three-dimensional world; the painter produces an imaginary depiction of what she or he sees from a set distance), the sculptor working in three dimensions was frequently tempted to move between the real and the imaginary (the sculptor produces a hybrid artefact, a curious amalgam of what is seen of the subject from a set distance, and of what is known of the subject from experience in the real world).

The result, notes Sartre, is a paradox:

> My real distance from the block of marble has become confused with my imaginarty distance from [the subject portrayed]. The properties of real space cover and mask those of imaginary space: in particular, the real divisibility of marble destroys the indivisibility of the person. (SIT3, p. 298)

Hence the impression of inert being, of lifeless cadavers, of juxtaposed, non-unified sculptural forms. Giacometti's originality, in Sartre's view, is to have avoided this classical confusion between the real and the imaginary, and to have situated his sculptures in an unequivocal imaginary space. In practical terms, this means that he produces his sculptures as if he were a painter; he creates his figures as he sees them at a set distance, with the result that however close one is situated to them, declares Sartre, the figures themselves retain this absolute distance from the onlooker:

> he places under our eyes a distant woman – who remains distant even were we to touch her with the tips of our fingers. The block of plaster is close to us, but the imaginary figure is distant. (SIT3, p. 302)

Giacometti's figures consequently remain at a respectful distance from the onlooker. They retain a certain mysterious aura, an undeniably enigmatic quality. The fleshy contours of the human form are sketched in, alluded to, suggested, but never fully revealed. It is this imaginary elusiveness which ultimately maintains them in a delicate balance between the in-itself of being and the for-itself of consciousness. Indeed, Sartre goes further. Giacometti's figures reveal to us man and woman as he or she is perceived by others, 'as a being whose essence is to exist for others' (SIT3, p. 302). 'As soon as I see them', notes Sartre, 'they spring up in my visual field as an idea in my consciousness' (SIT3, p. 301). Giacometti accordingly resolves the problem of the infinite divisibility of matter which reduces sculpted figures to an assemblage of juxtaposed parts by resorting to a systematic use of elongation. The series of fragile, delicately attenuated, almost spectral figures produced by Giacometti constitutes the material expression of human beings surging up in the world in a unified act. In this manner, Giacometti's figures avoid the petrification of being and gesture tantalisingly towards endowing inert material substance with an imaginary, fleeting existence.

These figures are also disturbing, Sartre alleges. They do not resemble the reassuringly inert statues of classical sculpture. They signify, on the contrary, an ill-defined human presence: 'Something has happened to these figures', remarks Sartre, echoing the 'At last something is happening to me' allegedly uttered by Giacometti at the moment of his car accident. 'Are [these figures] victims of concentration camps or are they insubstantial bodies rising gently heavenwards?' asks Sartre rhetorically (SIT3, p. 303). No matter, they draw us into their imaginary space and force us to reflect on the frailty of the human condition.

Sartre's account of Giacometti's paintings, 'Les Peintures de Giacometti', was published for the first time in May 1954. 'For five hundred years', notes Sartre, 'pictures have been filled to bursting point; the whole universe is crammed into them' (SIT4, p. 353). In the same way, therefore, that Sartre perceives Giacometti as revolutionising the artistic project of the sculptor by going back 3000 years, so he interprets Giacometti's painted canvases as a radical reorientation of the painting of the past 500 years. Unlike the paintings that Roquentin, for example, viewed in the Bouville Museum, Giacometti's work does not evoke a sense of order and stable being in the world. On the contrary, in Sartre's eyes, they allude ambiguously to the uncertainty of man's fragile existence. Just as Sartre maintained that Giacometti inverted traditional sculptural practice by shaping his figures as would a painter at a fixed and absolute distance from the onlooker, so, he argues, Giacometti inverts traditional painting practice by depicting his figures as would a sculptor, detaching them from any precise relationship with their surroundings. In the same way, Sartre contends, that Giacometti's aim as a sculptor is to inject a semblance of existence into the inert materiality from which the sculpted figure is formed, so his aim as a painter is to eliminate from the canvas an excess of being, and attempt in the process to evoke in painted form what Sartre refers to as 'the great universal Void', the reality of man's presence in the world.

Giacometti's ambition to transpose onto canvas the void at the heart of existence is achieved, according to Sartre, by a number of technical devices. In the first instance, the human figure is depicted alone, entirely disconnected from worldly surroundings. Not only is the excess of material being so fulsomely present in other paintings systematically eradicated from Giacometti's canvases, but also the human figures themselves are strangely set apart from whatever minimal environmental frame that might be visible. The human figure and the surroundings are separated by the void of existence.

Second, Sartre is at pains to stress the extent to which Giacometti makes use of lines in his paintings as centripetal forces discharging a multiplicity of movement leading back inevitably to the centre of the figure portrayed. Lines consequently do not function as boundary points delimiting figure from frame, container from contents, but rather as vectors of a dynamic network of forces. Just as the technique of elongation in Giacometti's sculpture imbues the sculptures themselves with a sense of burgeoning existence, thereby transcending the inert materiality of classical sculpture, so Sartre argues, the use of lines as centripetal forces in Giacometti's paintings, prevents the human figure from lapsing into the rock-like state of being of the dignitaries portrayed, for example, in the Bouville Museum.

Third, Giacometti makes specific use of white striations in his paintings as highlights to guide the eye, but which nonetheless remain the visible signs of the void at the heart of the painting itself. The underlying thrust of Sartre's argument is once again that these artistic techniques are subordinated to the global project of portraying the nothingness in which human beings are situated in order the more effectively to project a painted image of human existence in its indivisible and dynamic unity.

The overall impact of Giacometti's paintings is similarly disturbing. The hallucinatory impression that these paintings evoke is likened to the flickering images glimpsed in the flames of a fire. Sartre refers to the ambiguous, insubstantial quality as 'calculated indeterminacy' or 'overdeterminacy' (SIT4, p. 359). The elusive quality of Giacometti's paintings is both spellbinding and frustrating at the same time. The more we scrutinise a particular aspect of a painting, Sartre opines, the more elusive it becomes. What we see from the corner of our eye, on the other hand, appears for a fleeting instant to be both clear and unambiguous.

Sartre concludes by comparing Giacometti to a magician. When we look at his paintings, he argues, we are both taken in by and connive in his trickery. In the end, this is perhaps Sartre's definitive understanding of the artist: someone who creates an imaginary object with the intention of producing in the onlooker a real emotion. Whether it be by the production of elongated sculptural figures or striated, centripetally driven line paintings, Giacometti sets the onlooker an imaginary trap with the intention of provoking a real emotion. If Giacometti cannot achieve this, concludes Sartre, then nobody can.

TOTALISING CONCLUSIONS?

Sartre unquestionably held Giacometti in very high esteem. In Sartre's eyes, Giacometti's artistic project was located at the very roots of the sculptural and pictorial enterprise. Although, as the preceding analysis has highlighted, Sartre's interpretation of Giacometti's work is ideologically motivated, most notably his strategic ambition to downgrade early surrealist influences on Giacometti's work and to enhance phenomenological and existential aspects, it would nonetheless be totally misguided to dismiss Sartre's views because of their ideological bias. Sartre interrogates Giacometti's work on his own terms and the result is a rich, if partial, view of one of the most important artists in postwar Paris.

In 1972, Simone de Beauvoir made the following judgement of Giacometti's work: 'In my opinion his paintings and drawings became more impressive as the years went by. But as for his sculpture, his greatest period was during the postwar from 1945 until 1952.'[41] This value-judgement could be dismissed as strategic positioning, since it privileges precisely those works highlighted for special attention by Sartre in his critical essays. The 1991–2 Giacometti retrospective exhibition in Paris[42] appeared in my eyes, however, to confirm de Beauvoir's view. What the Paris exhibition achieved, and what Sartre's critical essays do not achieve, was to place the full range of Giacometti's work in perspective: from the first bust of Diego in 1914 to the final bust of Lotar in the 1960s. Viewing the totality of Giacometti's work in its chronological development in terms of theme, style and proportion was beneficial to the extent that it placed Sartre's highly original, but selective interpretation of Giacometti's creative output in context.

It also disclosed the enormous scope that there would have been for Sartre to develop his ideas on the life and work of Giacometti in far greater detail. In the interview with Michel Sicard Sartre asserted: 'Giacometti was someone who was far more complex than the picture that I have painted of him',[43] implying that had Sartre set his mind to it, a gigantic, totalising biography along the lines of his work on Genet and Flaubert would have been a real possibility. And yet, when all is said and done, it is perhaps fortunate, as Olivier Todd indicated at the Tate conference, that Sartre did not produce such a work, that he simply wrote the two short but highly original pieces that I have examined in the preceding pages, that as a consequence he brought Giacometti's work to the attention of the public at large, and that Giacometti himself was therefore not burdened or even possibly artistically sterilised, as was Jean Genet, by the overpowering presence of a potentially terrorising Sartrean biography of his artistic project.

9

Mediated Politics: Sartre and Chomsky Revisited

The preceding analysis has, I hope, shed light both on Sartre's political itinerary in the postwar period and on the manner in which his political and ideological views were reflected and refracted in specific cultural forms; initially in the traditional form of theatrical dramatisation, subsequently in the slightly more subversive ideologically critical art essay form. As I indicated at the outset of this book, the principal objective is not complete coverage of Sartre's work, rather representative selection of key components of his political and cultural outlook. Chapters 7 and 8, centred on the theatre and on art criticism, fall within the general category of 'traditional' cultural forms. In this final chapter, it would seem appropriate not merely to shift the focus of attention substantively from the 'traditional' to the 'newly emerging', but also to move beyond the conventional discourse of the academic monograph and formulate ideas on Sartre's progressive engagement with new audiovisual cultural forms in a different writing style.

The subject of this chapter is therefore the manner in which Sartre contends with the written and audiovisual media in postwar France.[1] However, rather than approach this task from the somewhat pedestrian and prosaic standpoint of the traditional academic monograph, I intend to offer my ideas in the shape of a series of news reports. In the same way that Sartre described his biography of Flaubert as a 'true novel',[2] a judicious mixture of fact and fiction, what follows is a series of semi-factual, semi-imaginary news reports in which fact and fiction coalesce. My intention, therefore, is to narrate a media story which, for the sake of symbolic clarity, I shall entitle: 'The Roads to Censorship'.

THE ROADS TO CENSORSHIP

In this media story there will be four primary characters:

1. The principal character is obviously **Jean-Paul Sartre** himself, previously designated as the most widely-studied, widely-researched intellectual of the twentieth century.
2. The second character is **Noam Chomsky**, Professor of Linguistics at MIT, referred to by the *New York Times* in the 1980s as 'arguably the most important intellectual alive today'. I have chosen to include Chomsky for three reasons:
   - (i) it seems to me that Chomsky's intellectual itinerary is remarkably and strangely similar to Sartre's – they are both dissident intellectuals, one from a French/European cultural background, the other from a North American cultural background;
   - (ii) Chomsky's American/Anglo-Saxon perspective is an instructive point of comparison for an English-speaking audience to Sartre's French/European standpoint; and
   - (iii) Chomsky has offered a coherent theory of the media which effectively illuminates the significance of Sartre's relations with the French press and audiovisual industry.
3. The third character is **Pierre Lazareff**, probably the most important and influential French press baron of the postwar period. Most notably, he was the chief executive of *France-Soir*, the newspaper which became during the 1950s the most widely read daily in France; in other words, Lazareff was the French Rupert Murdoch of the 1950s and 1960s.

4. The fourth and final character is **Charles de Gaulle**, President of France from 1958 to 1969, a statesman who, according to Edouard Balladur, a former French prime minister, 'unquestionably dominates this century'.[3] At the same time, as Chapter 3 amply demonstrated, de Gaulle was undoubtedly Sartre's principal political opponent in postwar France.

Sartre will of course play the central role in this media story. Chomsky will provide the theoretical underpinning to the argument. Lazareff and de Gaulle, two key social actors in opposition to Sartre's view of the world, will have walk-on parts designed to illustrate particular facets of Sartre's attitude to the media. The story will be in four segments, four interconnected news reports narrated by the media correspondent of a prominent European newspaper:

News report 1: Chomsky's Media Secrets
News report 2: Sartre Takes on the Press Barons
News report 3: Sartre's Radio Exploits
News report 4: Sartre Censored on Television

News Report 1: Chomsky's Media Secrets

The place is Toronto, Canada. The time is 1988. Noam Chomsky prepares to broadcast on Canadian television a programme entitled 'Manufacturing Consent – Thought Control in a Democratic Society' (referred to hereinafter as MC).[4] 'How do the media operate?', asks Chomsky rhetorically. 'What is the role and function of the media in contemporary democracies?' In the course of the programme Chomsky outlined a coherent and controversial theory of the media based on the idea of 'cultural indoctrination', in which the key terms are the 'manufacturing of consent' and the production of 'necessary illusions'.

'We live', noted Chomsky, 'entangled in webs of endless deceit, we live in a highly indoctrinated society where elementary truths are easily buried' (MC). The standard view of the media, he argued, the idea that the press, radio and television 'enable the public to assert meaningful control over the political process' (MC) is fundamentally flawed. Such a view is, for Chomsky, an illusion, a 'necessary illusion' designed to perpetuate the myth of democratic decision-making and social organisation. Indoctrination is consequently the very essence of democracy, maintained Chomsky, and the targets of such indoctrination are in the first instance the political class, the well-educated 20 per cent of the population and subsequently the remaining 80 per cent who are systematically encouraged merely to follow orders and not to think.

Chomsky's 'propaganda model' of the media therefore proposes that the primary function of a national press and audiovisual industry is to set a general agenda to which others adhere. This general agenda, in Chomsky's view, inevitably reflects the opinions and interests of the governing élites and corporations which own and control the media themselves. Through a sophisticated editorial process of 'selection of topics', 'distribution of concerns', 'emphasis', 'framing of issues', 'filtering of information', and most notably, 'bounding of the debate', the picture of the world presented by the media serves the interests of dominant groups.

The media therefore at one level set the agenda for the political class, and at another level dull the brains of the population at large through the dissemination and broadcasting of undisguised trivialities.

Perhaps the most striking feature of Chomsky's Toronto analysis was his account of the manner in which the bounds of acceptable debate are set. It is, of course, important to differentiate between the situation in the United States and the situation in Europe and in France in particular. The spectrum of ideological opinion is certainly narrower in the United States than in Europe, notably in the France of 1944–75 when Sartre's involvement in the media occurred. Nonetheless, the general principle of the bounding of the debate, that is to say, the setting up of fixed ideological parameters within which discussion can legitimately occur, is a useful one to retain.

As Chomsky alleged, anyone who transgresses these generally accepted ideological limits is immediately classified as a lunatic, someone who sounds as if she or he has just landed from another planet. This is particularly the case, he asserted, since the structural demands of the media (especially television) require that ideas be expressed concisely. With limited air-time at the broadcaster's disposal, concision is crucial, and the genius of this structural device for governing élites and programme-makers is that such brevity of expression enables only platitudes or conventional thoughts to be expressed via the medium itself.

Unconventional thoughts which inevitably shock need to be explained and justified. Since there is no time for such explanation and justification, the thoughts inevitably remain undeveloped and unjustified. They send shockwaves through the broadcasting system, but they are ultimately neutralised as the extreme aberrations of lunatic thought beyond the realm of the reasonable.

Chomsky offered several provocative examples of his own controversial assertions which have been marginalised as lunatic ideas by the American media. Fleeting images of Chomsky uttering the following two sentences flashed across a television screen:

(i) There is no more morality in public affairs today than there was at the time of Genghis Khan (MC)
(ii) Education is a system of imposed ignorance (MC)

Chomsky himself could not dispute the apparent lunacy of his own ideas when embodied in the evanescent images of a television screen. 'You can't give evidence and justify the unorthodox if you're stuck with concision', he opined. 'I agree with the broadcaster who said that I sounded as if I had just landed from the planet Neptune when I made these remarks on television' (MC).

The function of the media in Chomsky's system is, therefore, not to promote democratic debate; it is rather to deselect, to marginalise, to categorise as lunatic controversial thoughts of this kind. Chomsky insisted that his particular approach to the media based on a propaganda model cannot be refuted as simply yet another conspiracy theory. The propaganda model, he asserted, is based squarely on institutional analysis, that is to say analysis of the formal, political and economic structures of the media themselves, in short the 'political economy of the media'. His is not a form of academic whimpering about conspiratorial élites ganging up on the rest of us. No, in Chomsky's view, the media operate in a certain manner because they are structurally organised to serve the interests of specific powerful groups. 'What the media are doing', he argued, 'is ensuring that we do not act on our responsibilities, and that the interests of power are served, not the needs of the suffering' (MC).

The electoral success in the 1990s of Silvio Berlusconi, the Italian media magnate, an almost inevitable consequence of his access to the influence and power of television broadcasting, offers a striking example of precisely what Chomsky refers to as the 'manufacturing of consent'. Press reports, for example, of a leaked document from the immensely powerful Italian P2 Masonic Lodge with which Berlusconi had close links, highlighted: 'the need to build up private television ... to control public opinion'.[5]

News Report 2: Sartre Takes on the Press Barons

Listening to Noam Chomsky addressing a North American audience in 1988, notes our European media correspondent, I was reminded of the intellectual itinerary of Jean-Paul Sartre several decades earlier. Chomsky's ideas on the manner in which the media can distort through emphasis, concision and deselection, and can generally trivialise the democratic process echoed Sartre's personal experience of the French media between 1944 and 1975.

The place is Paris. The time is September 1975. Jean-Paul Sartre, Nobel Prize winner and leading French intellectual, today pulled out of a projected television history series for the second state broadcasting channel on the grounds that he had been censored by the French government, notably by the Gaullist Prime Minister, Jacques Chirac, and the Gaullist MP, Robert André Vivien. 'The government was afraid that I would say something lunatic on the state controlled television network', alleged Sartre.

We therefore publish in three parts an interview with Sartre explaining the nature of his relations with the media in the postwar period; to begin with: 'Sartre Takes on the Press Barons': 'I spent almost 25 years writing intermittently for the establishment press in France (44–68)' noted Sartre. 'It all began in 1944. I got my first taste of news reporting writing for *Combat* during the liberation of Paris. I described the day-to-day events as the Germans were expelled. Then Albert Camus and Raymond Aron suggested that I go to the United States and write news reports for *Combat* and *Le Figaro*. This was a great opportunity for me; so I took it.'

Sartre recalled with great relish his first report for *Le Figaro,* which had almost given Raymond Aron heart failure. '[Sartre] began his career as a journalist with a blunder that annoyed Aron', Simone de Beauvoir was later to note; 'he described the anti-Gaullism of the US leaders during the war with such willingness that he was nearly sent back to France'.[6]

These initial articles for *Le Figaro* are significant because they demonstrate not only the fact that from the outset Sartre was ready and willing to speak his mind on issues which other journalists might have treated with greater tact, but also the fact that Sartre's underlying political opposition to Gaullism was masked in 1945 by the image of de Gaulle as resistance leader and opponent of Pétain and Giraud.

'In the 1950s', Sartre continued, 'I wrote several poor quality articles on the Soviet Union for the pro-communist newspaper *Libération* (1954), and subsequently attacked de Gaulle in a series of articles in *L'Express* (1958)'. 'I was always opposed to de Gaulle's politics', Sartre insisted. 'They were at the other extreme to my idea of a democratic system. His conception of France was totally different from mine. I reproach myself for having been too respectful towards de Gaulle throughout my life ... I should have attacked him directly as a dangerous individual'.[7]

'During the 1960s I wrote initially a series of articles on Cuba for *France-Soir*, the biggest selling French daily newspaper of the time, 1.5 million copies per day, and owned by Pierre Lazareff. And then, I wrote principally for *Le Nouvel observateur* until 1968. I made a point of attacking colonialism in all its guises, notably in Vietnam. I continued my polemic with de Gaulle throughout the 60s, and in 1968 I publicly quarrelled with Raymond Aron, who seemed to have no idea what the events of May 68 signified'.

'After 1968', continued Sartre, 'I was gradually sucked into the revolutionary press, and I played a significant role between 1970 and 1973. My active involvement in the revolutionary press lasted in fact until the month of April 1973. This was the moment when we launched *Libération*, a new popular newspaper that we hoped would be free, no longer the plaything of publicity merchants and politicians, but a weapon in the struggle for total democracy and freedom'.[8] 'Unfortunately', noted Sartre, 'I became to all intents and purposes virtually blind at the same time, and this put an end to my writing career'.

I asked Sartre what stuck in his mind about his relations with the French press in the postwar period. 'Two incidents', he replied. The first was Lazareff, the second *La Cause du Peuple* and *Libération*.

'The Lazareff episode remains with me because it was symptomatic of relations between intellectuals and the media. Lazareff was the most important newspaper baron at the time. Even though the story of the French press in the postwar period is one of continual decline in the face of competition from the audiovisual industry, Lazareff succeeded in making *France-Soir* into the biggest selling daily newspaper of the 1950s'.

Sartre recalled his decision to take a trip to the Soviet Union in May and June 1954 at the height of the Cold War, when his links with the Soviet authorities were becoming closer. He had apparently spent a lot of time drinking vodka that summer. What with the Cold War and the vodka, he had somehow lost touch with the reality of the situation. He had also become very fond of the attractive woman who had been acting as his interpreter, Olga Graiavaka. The Cold War, the vodka, Olga Graiavaka, all had conspired to encourage him to write a piece for the pro-communist newspaper *Libération*: 'The USSR was a paradise on earth, the workers were all philosophers, critical freedom was total, the standard of living in the USSR was ceaselessly improving', and so on.

'After my first visit to the USSR in 1954, I lied', confessed Sartre. 'Lied is perhaps too grand a word. I wrote an article in which I said nice things about the USSR which I did not believe. After having just visited people, you can't start mud-slinging immediately on returning home; and in any case, I wasn't entirely sure where I stood in relation to the Soviet Union.[9] It was a complete fabrication. The one exception that proves the rule. Even at the height of the Cold War, I should not have compromised my commitment to telling the truth as I saw it'.

Pierre Lazareff had also visited the Soviet Union at the same time as Sartre. His view of the country had been quite different. He had written to *Libération*, protesting that Sartre's version of events was completely false. *Libération* had mockingly published Lazareff's letter as a sign of their commitment to free speech, arguing that Lazareff himself would be incapable of publishing left-wing ideas in the right-wing publications of his press empire. Sartre had then staged a successful coup against Lazareff a year later in 1955, satirising in his play *Nekrassov* the anti-communist bias of the French press. The allusions to Pierre Lazareff's *France-Soir* were inescapable.

That's why, six years later, in 1960, Sartre had thought of *France-Soir* when he visited Cuba. Why not challenge Lazareff again and see whether he would be capable of publishing Sartre's favourable account of Castro's revolutionary Cuban state? Lazareff had unexpectedly agreed, with the result that for two to three weeks in June and July 1960 Sartre became front-page news in the most popular of French daily newspapers: glossy photographs, lurid, populist headlines produced by Claude Lanzmann, the whole works. Lazareff had, of course, exploited the event to promote his newspaper as a forum of free expression, and to advise Sartre to re-assess his own highly critical opinion of the level of freedom of expression in the popular French press.

'My relations with Lazareff in the 1950s and 1960s', asserted Sartre, 'offer a striking image of the power struggle in France between intellectuals and media magnates for the hearts and minds of the public at large. In the decade or so that followed the war, intellectuals were definitely in the driving seat. Then, around the mid-1950s at the time of the production of *Nekrassov*, I think that the balance was tipped the other way, and media tycoons and press barons such as Lazareff gradually gained the upper hand in terms of influencing public opinion'.

'The second incident that sticks in my mind', continued Sartre, 'was my involvement in the revolutionary press, culminating in the launch of the new *Libération*. With the exception of the 1954 *Libération* incident (and it's important to differentiate between the pro-communist *Libération* of the 1950s and the radical, independent *Libération* of the 1970s), I have always attempted to tell the truth in as forthright a manner as possible', noted Sartre. There can be no doubting the fact that Sartre especially appreciated the plain-speaking of the editorials of the revolutionary press, the Maoist willingness to show no respect whatsoever for their political adversaries, a readiness to engage in violent verbal conflict with the representatives of the established order. Sartre was nonetheless not blind to the shortcomings of the revolutionary press, and he did not shirk from saying so, demonstrating in the process not merely that he cherished above all his own freedom of speech, but also that despite the 1954 *Libération* deviation, he subscribed to a fundamental code of ethics as a journalist: the search for the truth:

> What we have to do ... is to tell the truth, to say therefore: this has failed, and these are the reasons why; or else, in a given venture, this was successful and these are the reasons why. It is always better to tell the truth ... the establishment press tells the truth more often than the revolutionary press, even if it deceives. It deceives less. It deceives more skilfully. It manages to discredit whilst taking the facts into account. It is quite appalling to think that the revolutionary press is not superior in terms of truth to the establishment press, but rather inferior.[10]

'I shared the general political aims of the Maoists, but their revolutionary press publications frequently lacked credibility', affirmed Sartre. 'I considered it my moral duty to defend their right to free speech which was threatened by an oppressive Gaullist regime, but I also wanted to work towards a more effective news publication. The result was the new *Libération* launched in 1973, and I am proud of what this newspaper achieved, particularly in its early phase. In the end, however, I realised that to make any real impact on public opinion it was necessary to gain access to radio and television broadcasting and this was much more problematical for a traditional liberal intellectual such as myself'.

News Report 3: Sartre's Radio Exploits

In the aftermath of the censoring of Sartre's proposed television history series, Sartre continues his account of his relations with the media in the postwar period. He now turns his attention to radio broadcasting.

'The difficulty with gaining access to radio broadcasting in France was that the whole system was a state controlled monopoly', asserted Sartre. 'In 1947, I thought that it might be possible to make inroads in the system at a time when existentialism was very popular and when I was being courted by all the media. However, although I made over thirty broadcasts in all on French state radio, there were always obstacles or devices which somehow prevented me from saying precisely what I thought'.

The most striking example was the series of radio programmes that were broadcast in 1947 under the title of 'La Tribune des *Temps Modernes*'. 'I remember it in particular', noted Sartre, 'because it was the cause of my estranged relationship with Raymond Aron. He sided with the Gaullists who attacked me personally after the first broadcast.'

'Initially, I thought that we had succeeded in creating a genuine forum for free speech on the radio. We were a group of free-minded intellectuals owing allegiance to no-one but ourselves, and opening up the airwaves to dissenting, anti-establishment views. And we certainly annoyed a lot of people with these broadcasts. We were violently attacked after the programmes by the Gaullists on the Right and by the communists on the Left, and my experience has always taught me that if you're violently attacked by your political enemies, then you must be doing something right. It was the beginning of the Cold War. Everything was polarised. The discussion became abusive and somewhat personal on occasions. During the first broadcast on Gaullism, for example, one of the *Temps Modernes* group, Bonafé, drew a comparison between Charles de Gaulle as portrayed in an RPF political poster and Adolf Hitler. Two prominent Gaullists, Henry Torres and General Guillain de Bénouville, attacked me personally in the crudest of terms after the broadcast. Aron supported them rather than me, and that was the end of our friendship'.

In 1947 Sartre had been resolute in his defence of the 'Tribune des *Temps Modernes*' as a forum for free expression. The fact that the government of Robert Schuman, which replaced that of Paul Ramadier in November 1947, immediately censored the *Temps Modernes* radio broadcasts was the ultimate proof in Sartre's eyes that they had fulfilled their function of disinterested critical enquiry. The communist Pierre Hervé, however, had been much more sceptical. 'This ridiculous coup', he argued, 'which consisted in getting the urchin Jean-Paul Sartre to cause a stir, was organised by the Machiavellian Ramadier. Poor little innocent, how they have made use of you in their grand designs of state'.[11] 'Hervé was right', concluded Sartre. 'The government of the day had wanted to unleash a few well-known intellectuals against the communists.[12] We said what we wanted to say, but in the end Ramadier succeeded in manipulating us to serve his own political ends'.

'After my experience of radio broadcasting in the 1940s I became much more wary of the state monopoly. It's very easy to be drawn into their political agenda', argued Sartre. 'I gave a number of interviews in the 1950s and 1960s, but I only really ventured back into the system in 1973 for a "Radioscopie" interview with Jacques Chancel; and I did this for specific political purposes. Chancel had his own agenda: a cosy literary chat with a celebrated international philosopher. I had my agenda: to publicise the launch of the new popular daily newspaper, *Libération*. Chancel tried at one point to argue that my presence on his programme was a sign of the liberalism of the state broadcasting system. It was nothing of the kind. It was simply a convenient arrangement for them and for me.[13] The important thing is to set the agenda; otherwise your views are neutralised in their anodine programming formats'.

'The situation is even worse with television', Sartre continued.

News Report 4: Sartre Censored on Television

'When Georges Pompidou referred in 1972 to French television broadcasting as the "Voice of France",[14] he was not exaggerating', remarked Sartre. 'From the very beginning television was used by de Gaulle as a privileged means of communicating with the electorate, and the Gaullist party machine had no intention of letting anyone else have access to it, particularly if you wanted to express controversial views that would upset government sensibilities'.

Sartre had only ever appeared once on French state television: in 1969. Following the departure of de Gaulle and the election of Georges Pompidou in 1969, the new Prime Minister, Jacques Chaban Delmas had set in motion a process of audiovisual reform by establishing autonomous information units for each of the two television channels, one of which came under the jurisdiction of Pierre Desgraupes, a left-wing sympathiser. Desgraupes entrusted the weekly broadcast 'Panorama' to Olivier Todd, who invited Sartre to appear on the programme in December 1969.[15]

Sartre's acceptance of the invitation was surprising given that he had consistently refused to appear on French television since the early 1960s, not wishing to lend his support in any way to the government broadcasting monopoly. It is quite significant, in fact, that Sartre's boycott of French television coincided almost exactly with de Gaulle's period of presidential power. With de Gaulle gone and the ORTF authorities initiating reforms in information dissemination and current affairs programmes, Sartre judged the moment opportune to venture into the French state television service.

Sartre grasped the opportunity offered to him to formulate an unequivocal condemnation of the US presence in Vietnam, explicitly drawing an analogy between Hitler's extermination of the Jews and American 'genocide' of the Vietnamese people.[16] The analogy had been striking and provocative, and Sartre had doubtless felt at the time that he had made the point that he was trying to get across. But framed within a concise audiovisual format, Sartre's ideas had doubtless had an aura of lunacy about them when they were expressed in 1969.

So, we arrived finally at the conclusion of Sartre's audiovisual itinerary. Paris, 1975, and the projected television history series that had been censored by the Chirac government. Once again, Sartre's interest in television broadcasting had been prompted by audiovisual reforms set in motion by the recently elected President Valéry Giscard d'Estaing.

'We were approached', said Sartre, 'by Marcel Jullian, the Director-General of the Second channel in September 1974, who offered us the chance of producing a series of 10 television programmes of an hour and a quarter each on the history of the twentieth century, using my intellectual itinerary as a focus. We worked for a year and produced a 30-page synopsis and a short publicity film for the series itself. The series would have been a controversial document because it would have issued a direct challenge to right-wing, establishment histories of the twentieth century. It would, in particular, have stood in direct opposition to the traditional Gaullist vision of France and her role in the world. This is why the Gaullists, Chirac and Vivien, were overtly hostile to the series from the outset. They pretended that the series had failed to materialise for technical and financial reasons (they even maintained that I was trying to make a personal financial profit from the series); but the real reason was political censorship. They were afraid that I would say something lunatic on their state-run television network.

'In particular, they were afraid of what I would say during the last 15 minutes of each broadcast. The original idea was that each one hour programme would be followed by a 15 minute segment in which I would have the opportunity to comment freely on contemporary political events. The thought of giving me the opportunity to express freely and publicly my views on the right-wing regime in France simply terrified them, and they had to dream up a series of tactical manoeuvres to censor the series. I will not appear on French television again', concluded Sartre.

THE END OF THE STORY

What does this tale of Sartre's relations with the French press and radio and television broadcasting in postwar

France signify? It would appear to signify above all else the continuing importance and relevance of the debate on freedom of expression and censorship of the media. Since the death of Sartre in 1980, the social, political and cultural environment of France has profoundly changed: the Mitterrand experience after 1981 led to a fundamental reappraisal of the underlying premises of the socialist project, and a reluctant but inevitable acceptance by the Left of the market economy; the state broadcasting monopoly has been largely dismantled following the audiovisual reforms of 1986 and 1989 – deregulation and privatisation are now the buzzwords and catchphrases of the day in media circles; and, of course, the collapse of communism has brought with it not only a disaffection with ideology, but also a fundamental realignment, almost a redefinition of the intellectual class itself. The moment of Sartre's death in 1980 is highly symbolic in this respect. And in many ways, Sartre's funeral, when 50 000 people spontaneously took to the streets of Paris in what Claude Lanzmann described as the 'last demonstration of May 1968',[17] marked the end of an era.

Since Sartre's death, and because of the far-reaching economic, social, political and perhaps above all technological changes of the 1980s and 1990s, the very terms of the debate about the media have altered. The issue at stake is no longer principally freedom of expression versus censorship. This traditional debate which was linked to ideological and political issues has been replaced by a newer, more technocratic, more technologically-orientated debate: 'market competitiveness versus the defence of French culture'. The 1990s GATT negotiations in which the French government defended the French audiovisual industry for both economic and cultural reasons witnessed a distinct shift of emphasis that doubtless reflected the agenda set by governing élites. As a consequence, issues of political empowerment at grass-roots level which are at the heart of the debate on freedom of expression versus censorship are now inevitably masked and neglected.

It would, however, be both rash and misguided to consign this particular debate to the nether regions of history. Despite the greater emphasis currently being given to the issues of market performance and the defence of national cultural specificities, the freedom of expression–censorship debate retains its potency today in technological societies where the scope for media control and manipulation is increasing exponentially. The continuing topicality and relevance of this old debate is the principal reason why I have used this opportunity to place the work of Chomsky in relation to the work of Sartre. The theoretical insights of Chomsky and the practical experience of Sartre offer an illuminating case-study of the way in which two important civil libertarians have responded to the challenge of the media in contemporary democracies.

I would like to finish with two quotations and one anecdote. The quotations simply reiterate the fundamental idea of the importance of freedom of expression. The first is by George Orwell. Writing at the height of the Second World War, Orwell declared:

> If liberty means anything at all, it means the right to tell people what they do not want to hear.[18]

The second is by Chomsky. In 1988 Chomsky stretched his argument to the very limits by defending the right of the French right-wing ideologue, Roger Faurisson, to express the view that the holocaust was a figment of everyone's imagination:

> I'm saying that if you believe in freedom of speech, then you believe in freedom of speech for views that you *don't* like. Goebbels was in favour of freedom of speech for views that he liked. So was Stalin. If you're in favour of freedom of speech, that means you're in favour of freedom of speech precisely for views that you despise.

> Otherwise, you're not in favour of freedom of speech. There are two positions that you can have on freedom of speech, and you can decide which position you want. With regards to my defence of the utterly offensive, of people who express utterly offensive views, I haven't the slightest doubt that every commissar says: 'You're defending that person's views'. No, I'm not. I'm defending his right to express them. The difference is crucial, and has been understood outside of fascist circles since the eighteenth century.[19]

The final word must, of course, be with Sartre. Sartre was throughout his life fascinated by what he refers to in technical language as 'counter-finality' (*la contre-finalité*), the unpredictable quirks of history which transform individual and social projects into outcomes that are totally alien to the agents of the projects themselves. In his preface to the autobiography of André Gorz, written in 1958,[20] Sartre recounts a science-fiction story that he had found particularly appealing, since it seemed to him to sum up the structural dynamics of personal and social relations. It is the story of human beings landing on the planet Venus, triumphantly seeking out in typically arrogant and colonial fashion the Venusians, their intended extra-terrestrial colonial victims. Very soon, however, their triumph is transformed into despair when the conquerors realise that the Venusians are invisible to the human eye and have led them into a trap. The would-be conquerors, after being imprisoned in a glass cage, are then subjected to intelligence tests by the natural inhabitants of the planet Venus, whom they thought they would subjugate to their will. The testers were in the end tested, the manipulators manipulated.

Sartre sees in this science-fiction story of role-reversal the image of the contemporary human condition, a dialectic between domination and subservience at the core of our existential selves. I, on the other hand, prefer to see in it an image of the relations between the media and the public, where those who are initially classified as extra-terrestrial beings uttering lunatic thoughts from an alien planet (Sartre and Chomsky) are more likely than not to be the very people who are subjecting the media colonisers themselves to intelligence tests in order to bring enlightenment to their fellow beings.

Postscript: A Final Word on Sartre

Speaking of Sartre ten years after his death, Benny Lévy noted: 'I have never met anyone with such a capacity to call himself into question'.[1] This willingness to engage in self-criticism, this commitment to seek out new ways of interpreting the world, this refusal to envisage the status quo as unchangeable, this resilient conviction that self-renewal and self-improvement are always a human possibility, would appear to me to be at the heart of the continuing fascination and relevance of Sartre's life and work. At the end of an itinerary through the work of Sartre that has lasted 30 years, this for me is the final word on Sartre.

Whatever else Sartre may or may not epitomise, one thing is certain: however limited the possibilities for freedom might be, individuals are, according to Sartre, always ultimately responsible for their acts and for the shaping of their lives. Freedom, in other words, cannot be given, it must be gained in a process of struggle. Consequently, all forms of knowledge that are synonymous with the passive transmission and reception of ideas are ultimately suspect in Sartre's eyes, since they do not engage individual consciousness in a ceaseless critical debate about the nature and legitimacy of knowledge itself. Everything that has been examined in the preceding pages of this book, everything that I have written on Sartre, constitutes a testimony to a primary and fundamental assertion made by Sartre at the height of the events of May 1968, an assertion that in my view encapsulates precisely the legacy of the Sartrean project to the contemporary world:

> *Knowledge which is not constantly criticized, transcending itself and reaffirming itself in the light of such criticism, has no value ... The only way to learn is to protest.*[2]

English Translation of the Principal Titles Cited in French

Avant-propos à Aden Arabie	*Foreword to Aden Arabia*
La Cause du Peuple	*The Cause of the People*
'Les Communistes et la paix'	'The Communists and Peace'
Les Communistes ont peur de la révolution	*The Communists are afraid of the Revolution*
Les Chemins de la liberté (trilogy)	*The Roads to Freedom*
(i) *L'Age de raison*	*The Age of Reason*
(ii) *Le Sursis*	*The Reprieve*
(iii) *La Mort dans l'âme*	*Iron in the Soul*
Critique de la raison dialectique	*Critique of Dialectical Reason*
La Dernière Chance	*The Last Chance*
Le Diable et le bon dieu	*The Devil and the Good Lord*
'Drôle d'amitié'	'An Odd Friendship'
Entretiens sur la politique	*Debating Politics*
L'Etre et le néant	*Being and Nothingness*
L'Existentialisme est un humanisme	*Existentialism and Humanism*
'Le Fantôme de Staline'	'The Ghost of Stalin'
L'Idiot de la famille	*The Family Idiot*
J'Accuse	*I Accuse*
Jean sans terre	*Rootless John*
Libération	*Liberation*
Les Mots	*Words*
La Nausée	*Nausea*
Nekrassov	*Nekrassov*
On a raison de se révolter	*Rebellion is justified*
Orphée noir	*Black Orpheus*
Préface: Les Damnés de la Terre	*Preface: The Wretched of the Earth*
'Présentation des *Temps Modernes*'	'Introducing *Modern Times*'

Qu'est-ce que la littérature?	*What is Literature?*
Réflexions sur la question juive	*On the Jewish Question*
Saint Genet, comédien et martyr	*Saint Genet, Actor and Martyr*
Les Séquestrés d'Altona	*The Condemned of Altona*
Situations	*Situations*
Les Temps Modernes	*Modern Times*
Les Troyennes	*The Trojan Women*
'Visages'	'Faces'

Notes and References

PREFACE

1. M. Contat and M. Rybalka, *Sartre: Bibliographie 1980–1992* (CNRS Editions, 1993).
2. 'Paris Postwar: Art and Existentialism 1945–55', Tate Gallery, London, 9 June–5 September 1993. See Chapter 8.
3. Interview with K. Tynan, *Observer*, 18 and 21 June 1961; reprinted in TDS, pp. 152–68.

1 INITIAL THOUGHTS

1. M. Scriven, *Sartre's Existential Biographies* (London: Macmillan, 1984).
2. M. Scriven, *Sartre and the Media* (London: Macmillan, 1993).
3. M. Scriven, *Paul Nizan: Communist Novelist* (London: Macmillan, 1988).
4. See for example: M.-A. Burnier, *Les Existentialistes et la politique* (Gallimard, 1966); A. Dobson, *Jean-Paul Sartre and the Politics of Reason* (Cambridge: Cambridge University Press, 1993); W. McBride, *Sartre's Political Theory* (Bloomington and Indianapolis: Indiana University Press, 1991).
5. See for example: C. Howells, *Sartre's Theory of Literature* (London: Modern Humanities Research Association, 1979); R. Goldthorpe, *Sartre: Literature and Theory* (Cambridge: Cambridge University Press, 1984); G. Bauer, *Sartre and the Artist* (Chicago: University of Chicago Press, 1969).

2 SARTREAN POLITICS: TRANSITION AND DIVISION

1. J.-B. Pontalis, in M. Contat and J. Lecarme, 'Les Années Sartre', radio programme broadcast on France Culture on 24 and 25 August 1990.
2. 'Jean-Paul Sartre on his Autobiography', interview with O. Todd, *Listener*, 6 June 1957, p. 915.
3. Ibid.

4. P. Nizan, '*Les Violents* par Ramon Fernandez', *Monde*, 1 August 1935.
5. R. Debray, in M. Contat and J. Lecarme, 'Les Années Sartre', radio programme broadcast on France Culture, 24 and 25 August 1990.
6. J.-P. Sartre, D. Rousset and G. Rosenthal, *Entretiens sur la politique* (Gallimard, 1949), p. 159.
7. For a detailed account of Sartre's political and cultural evolution during the 1945–55 Cold War period see: M. Scriven, 'Cold War Polarisation and Cultural Productivity in the Work of Sartre', *French Cultural Studies*, vol. 8, pt 1 (1997), pp. 117–26.
8. See the series of newspaper articles written by Sartre for *Le Figaro* and *Combat* in 1945, listed in M. Scriven, *Sartre and the Media* (London: Macmillan, 1993), pp. 139–40.
9. Published initially in *Les Temps Modernes*, nos 81 (July 1952), 84–5 (October–November 1952) and 101 (April 1954); 'Les Communistes et la paix' was reprinted in SIT6, pp. 80–384.
10. See the series of articles written by Sartre for *Libération* in 1954, listed in M. Scriven, *Sartre and the Media* (London: Macmillan, 1993), p. 140.
11. Published initially in *Les Temps Modernes*, nos 129–31 (November–December 1956 and January 1957); 'Le Fantôme de Staline' was reprinted in SIT7, pp. 144–307.
12. See 'La Tribune des *Temps Modernes*: Le Gaullisme et le RPF', radio programme broadcast 20 October 1947.
13. See the articles written by Sartre for *L'Express* in 1958, listed in M. Scriven, *Sartre and the Media* (London, Macmillan, 1993), p. 140.
14. J.-P. Sartre, *Les Communistes ont peur de la révolution* (Editions John Didier, 1969).
15. 'Autoportrait à soixante-dix ans', SIT10, pp. 197–8.

3 SARTRE AND DE GAULLE: TWO CONCEPTIONS OF FRANCE

1. Sartre died on 15 March 1980.
2. De Gaulle died in November 1970; he was born in November 1890.

3. 'Sartre: un colloque du groupe d'études sartriennes', Vidéothèque de Paris, 22–4 juin 1990; 'De Gaulle à l'écran', Vidéothèque de Paris, 26 juin–17 juillet 1990.
4. C. de Gaulle, *Mémoires de guerre: L'Appel 1940–1942* (Plon, 1954), p. 7.
5. C. de Gaulle, 'Discours au Parlement de Westminster, 7 April 1960'; cited in J. Lacouture, *Citations au Président de Gaulle* (Seuil, 1968), p. 80.
6. 'Justice and the State', in *Sartre in the Seventies: Interviews and Essays* (London: André Deutsch, 1978), pp. 175–6.
7. 'Elections: A Trap for Fools', in *Sartre in the Seventies: Interviews and Essays*, p. 204.
8. Jean-Paul Sartre, 'Un jour de victoire parmi les balles', *Combat*, 4 September 1944, p. 2.
9. See: C. de Gaulle, *Mémoires de guerre: L'Appel 1940–42* (Plon, 1954); *Mémoires de guerre: L'Unité 1942–44* (Plon, 1956).
10. Jean-Paul Sartre, 'La France vue d'Amérique', *Le Figaro*, 24 January 1945, p. 2.
11. See: *New York Times*, 25 January 1945 and 1 February 1945.
12. Jean-Paul Sartre, 'Victoire de gaullisme', *Le Figaro*, 25 January 1945, p. 2.
13. This first broadcast was reproduced *in extenso* under the title 'De Gaulle et le "gaullisme"', in *L'Order de Paris*, 22 October 1947, pp. 1 and 3.
14. Jean-Paul Sartre, 'Les bastilles de Raymond Aron', *Le Nouvel observateur*, 19–25 June 1968, reprinted in SIT8, pp. 175–92.
15. 'Le Prétendant', *L'Express*, no. 362 (22 May 1958; reprinted SIT5, pp. 89–101); 'La constitution du mépris', *L'Express*, no. 378 (11 September 1958; reprinted SIT5, pp. 102–12); 'Les grenouilles qui demandent un roi', *L'Express*, no. 380 (25 September 1958; reprinted SIT5, pp. 113–44); 'L'analyse du référendum', interview in *L'Express*, no. 499 (4 January 1961; reprinted SIT5, pp. 145–59).
16. Jean-Paul Sartre, 'Le Prétendant', SIT5, p. 96.
17. Ibid, SIT5, p. 100.
18. Jean-Paul Sartre, 'La constitution du mépris', SIT5, p. 102.

19. Jean-Paul Sartre, 'L'analyse du référendum', SIT5, p. 155.
20. Jean-Paul Sartre, 'Les grenouilles qui demandent un roi', SIT5, p. 155.
21. The initial version of Sartre's autobiography, entitled *Jean sans terre*, was written in 1953 and 1954. Sartre apparently shelved the manuscript for several years until 1961, when, prompted by a shortage of money, he decided to finalise the text for Gallimard. The redrafting of the autobiography therefore took place between 1961 and 1963.
22. Sartre worked on the film script of the life of Freud from 1958–60. The work was published by Gallimard in 1978 under the title *Le Scénario Freud*.
23. See in this respect the television programme produced by Michel Favart entitled 'Sartre contre Sartre' and broadcast on 25 and 28 September and 1 October 1990 on La Sept and FR3. Despite Sartre's increasingly hostile attitude to de Gaulle during the Algerian crisis, it needs to be noted that at the moment of the 'Affaire des 121' in 1960, de Gaulle is alleged to have protected Sartre from facing criminal charges on the grounds that 'one does not arrest Voltaire'; see ES2, p. 47.
24. See: ES, pp. 445–9 and 454–6; and Jean-Paul Sartre, 'Vietnam: Le Tribunal', in SIT8, pp. 7–124.
25. 'Lettre au Président de la République', SIT8, pp. 42–3; 'Réponse du Président de la République', SIT8, pp. 43–5; 'Sartre à de Gaulle', *Le Nouvel observateur*, 26 April 1967; reprinted in SIT8, pp. 46–57.
26. Jean-Paul Sartre, 'Sartre à de Gaulle', SIT8, pp. 49–50. Despite their disagreements over the Russell Tribunal, Sartre's postwar anti-Americanism ultimately echoed de Gaulle's own anti-American sentiments. See O. Todd, *Un fils rebelle* (Grasset, 1981), p. 201.
27. Ibid., pp. 50–1.
28. Jean-Paul Sartre, 'L'alibi', *Le Nouvel observateur*, no. 1 (19 November 1960; reprinted in SIT8, pp. 143–4).
29. (i) 'L'imagination au pouvoir', interview between Jean-Paul Sartre and Daniel Cohn-Bendit, *Le Nouvel observateur*, special supplement, 20 May 1968; (ii) 'Les bastilles

de Raymond Aron', *Le Nouvel observateur*, 19–25 June 1968, reprinted in SIT8, pp. 175–92; (iii) 'L'ideé neuve de mai 1968', *Le Nouvel observateur*, 26 June 1968, reprinted in SIT8, pp. 193–207; (iv) 'Il n'y a pas de bon gaullisme', *Le Nouvel observateur*, 4–10 November 1968, reprinted in SIT8, pp. 226–32.

30. 'Les bastilles de Raymond Aron', SIT8, p. 192.
31. 'Il n'y a pas de bon gaullisme', SIT8, p. 227.
32. See: P. Gavi, Jean-Paul Sartre and P. Victor, *On a raison de se révolter* (Gallimard, 1974), pp. 63–5.
33. See M. Scriven, 'Sartre attiré et repoussé par la télévision', *Les Temps Modernes,* nos 531–3 (October–December 1990), pp. 1072–95.
34. Cited in J.-D. Wolfromm, 'Qui avait peur de Jean-Paul Sartre?', *Le Matin de Paris*, 3 July 1980, p. 34.
35. See: (i) M. Clavel, 'Mon témoignage sur l'affaire Sartre', *Le Nouvel observateur*, 6 October 1975, p. 37; (ii) J.-D. Wolfromm, 'Qui avait peur de Jean-Paul Sartre?'.
36. R.-A. Vivien, in F. Mitterrand, *Sartre: une vie*, television programme broadcast on Antenne 2, 15 April 1990.
37. Synopsis, '75 ans d'histoire par ceux qui l'ont faite', p. 22. On p. 12 reference is made to 'Charles de Gaulle's appeal of 18 June', on p. 14 'Gaullism [which] sets up a cossetted state apparatus in London', on p. 18 to 'anger and despondency after de Gaulle's coup d'état of May 1958', and on p. 20 to an alleged remark by de Gaulle: 'Even if Jean-Paul Sartre were to go stark naked on the Champs Elysées, I would not arrest him'. This latter comment is clearly an ironic reference to de Gaulle's remark made in 1960 that 'one does not arrest Voltaire'.
38. Interview with Benny Lévy, 20 March 1990.
39. P. Gavi, Jean-Paul Sartre and P. Victor, *On a raison de se révolter* (Gallimard, 1974), p. 63.
40. 'M. Jean-Paul Sartre s'explique et polémique avec M. Marcel Jullian', *Le Monde*, 27 September 1975, p. 23.
41. B. Levy in F. Mitterrand, *Sartre: une vie,* television programme broadcast on Antenne 2, 15 April 1990. Interestingly and paradoxically, Olivier Todd perceives a fundamental similarity between Sartre and de Gaulle in what he describes as their mutual exploitation of a

mystifying rhetoric; in Sartre's case in the philosophical domain, in de Gaulle's case in the political sphere. See [illegible], *Un fils rebelle* (Grasset, 1981), pp. 199–200.

4 SARTRE AND THE NIZAN AFFAIR: THE COLD WAR POLITICS OF FRENCH COMMUNISM

1. Interview with Michel Contat, 22 June 1991.
2. L. Siegel, *La Clandestine* (Maren Sell, 1988).
3. See J.-P. Sartre, *Les Carnets de la drôle de guerre* (Gallimard, 1983), pp. 310–18, and n. 10.
4. Interview with Liliane Siegel, 21 June 1991.
5. Simone de Beauvoir, *Entretiens avec Jean-Paul Sartre* (Gallimard, 1981), p. 352.
6. J.-P. Sartre and M. Contat, 'Autoportrait à soixante-dix ans', *Le Nouvel observateur*, 7–13 July 1975, p. 70; reprinted in SIT10, pp. 133–226.
7. Ibid., pp. 191–2.
8. J.-P. Sartre, 'La Semence et Le Scaphandre', in *Ecrits de jeunesse* (edited by M. Contat and M. Rybalka, Gallimard, 1990), pp. 137–87. The first chapter was originally published in *Le Magazine Littéraire*, no. 59 (December 1971), pp. 29 and 59–64.
9. G. Idt, '*Les Chemins de la liberté*: Les Toboggans du romanesque', *Sartre inédit, Obliques*, nos 18–19 (1979).
10. J. Cau, in M. Contat and J. Lecarme, 'Les Années Sartre', radio programme broadcast on France Culture, 24 and 25 August 1990.
11. For the record, it is worth noting that Cau's comments on Sartre's relationship with his male intellectual peers need to be viewed in conjunction with his assessment of Sartre's relationships with women:

    > Women revealed to him an amusing and slightly irresponsible world which he found entertaining ... he considered a woman as the other who should be treated with great leniency. Sartre was moreover prepared to forgive most things to anyone who was in any way alienated, whether a Jew, a black, a woman.

But he did not really like women because he was extremely macho. ('Les Années Sartre')

12. It is, of course, important to differentiate between the level of their commitment to the PCF. Nizan was much more willing to submit to a party line: 'Nizan's allegiance to the party prevented him from seeing his radicalism through to the end', notes Sartre (SIT10, p. 194). Equally, Sartre insists that his was a fundamentally anarchistic outlook on life: 'I never accepted any authority over me, and I always considered that anarchy, that is to say a society without authority, could be achieved' (SIT10, p. 156).
13. For a more detailed account of Nizan's departure from the PCF, see M. Scriven, *Paul Nizan: Communist Novelist* (London: Macmillan, 1988), pp. 57–71.
14. M. Thorez, 'The Traitors in the Pillory', *The Communist International*, no. 3 (March 1940), pp. 171–8.
15. Ibid., pp. 177–8.
16. Ibid., p. 174. Two days after the banning of *l'Humanité* on 25 August 1939, Nizan had advocated communist collaboration on non-communist newspapers.
17. Ibid., p. 176.
18. H. Lefebvre, *L'Existentialisme* (Sagittaire, 1946).
19. L. Aragon, *Les Communistes 1: février–septembre 1939* (La Bibliothèque française, 1949).
20. S. Téry, *Beaux enfants qui n'hésitez pas* (Editeurs français réunis, 1957).
21. R. Garaudy, 'Garaudy, celui qui ne regrette rien', *Le Nouvel observateur*, 29 October–4 November 1979, pp. 111–53.
22. A. Rossi, *Physiologie du parti communist français* (Editions Self, 1948).
23. Ibid., pp. 400–1. Rossi quotes and paraphrases Dimitrov's argument as expressed in an article published in a widely circulated PCF tract entitled: *La Vérité sur la guerre: comment la gagner*. He refers specifically to Nizan on pages 257–8, 338 (n. 1), 356 (n. 2) and 442–3. See also A. Rossi, *Les Communistes français pendant le drôle de guerre* (Les Iles d'Or, 1951), pp. 40, 42 (n. 27) and 254.

24. See P. Daix, *J'ai cru au matin* (Robert Laffont, 1976), p. 340 n. 1: 'Party intellectuals had spread the rumour that Sartre was not above suspicion. Moreover, Sartre had always been the friend of Nizan, considered by the Party to be a police informer following his resignation over the Nazi–Soviet pact'. See also D. Caute, *Communism and the French Intellectuals: 1914–1960* (London: André Deutsch, 1964), p. 151.
25. G. Steiner, 'Sartre: The Suspect Witness', *The Times Literary Supplement*, 3 May 1991, pp. 3–5. Steiner notes:

> The Sartre–Beauvoir attitudes during the Occupation verge on the nauseating. It is not only Sartre's repeated findings that there had never been so quiet, so favourable a time for sound intellectual and creative labours, or his sardonic observation that events were causing the beneficial disappearance of many bores and busybodies. It is Sartre's self-serving omissions in the hours of agony, his refusal to sign an appeal condemning the removal of undesirables from academic and public posts lest any such signatures endanger the forthcoming première of *Les Mouches*. It is Sartre's tacit (?) accord with German censorship and with the staging of the play in the Théâtre Sarah Bernard – whose famous name had, of course, been withdrawn and altered under Nazi racial edicts.

Sartre himself maintained that the German occupying forces were not particularly concerned by the activities of writers and artists and chose rather to concentrate their repressive efforts on armed resistance fighters: 'it would have been more damaging and dangerous to arrest Eluard or Mauriac than to let them whisper in freedom. The Gestapo undoubtedly preferred to concentrate its efforts on clandestine forces and on resistance fighters whose real acts of destruction were a far greater cause for concern than our abstract negativity' (SIT2, p. 328, n. 13).

26. R. Garaudy, 'Un faux prophète: Jean-Paul Sartre', *Les Lettres françaises*, 28 December 1945, p. 1.

27. J.-P. Sartre, 'Matérialisme et révolution', *Les Temps Modernes*, no. 9 (June 1946), pp. 1537–63; no. 10 (July 1946), pp. 1–32; reprinted in SIT3, pp. 135–225.
28. A. A. Zhdanov, *The International Situation* (London: W. P. Coates, 1947).
29. Cited in L. Casanova, *Le Parti communiste, les intellectuels et la nation* (Editions Sociales, 1949), p. 9.
30. Ibid., pp. 32–3.
31. Ibid., p. 8.
32. J.-P. Sartre, *Qu'est-ce que la littérature?* (Gallimard, 1948; SIT2); initially published in five parts in *Les Temps Modernes*, nos 17–22 (February–July 1947). Significantly, the July 1947 number contained not only the final part of *Qu'est-ce que la littérature?*, including an uncompromising attack on the cultural policy of the PCF ('Stalinist communist politics are incompatible with the honest practice of the literary profession' [p. 87]), but also accounts of the Nizan Affair (pp. 181–4) and the Heidegger Affair (pp. 115–38).
33. La Tribune des *Temps Modernes*, 'Communisme et anticommunisme', radio programme broadcast on 27 October 1947.
34. J. Kanapa, *L'Existentialisme n'est pas un humanisme* (Editions Sociales, 1947). Kanapa refers specifically to the Nizan Affair in the following terms:

    > Just as Marcel, with the Church, reserves his appeals for charity solely for war criminals and condemned fascists, so Sartre commits himself solely to 'bad causes'; since all activities are equivalent, why not instigate a 'Nizan Affair'? It seems that for the existentialists all activities are indeed equivalent ... except one which is worthy of attention: saving traitors. (p. 74)

35. The signatories of the statement which appeared in *Littérature*, *Combat*, *Carrefour* and *Gavroche* were: R. Aron, G. Adam, A. Breton, S. de Beauvoir, P. Bost, A. Billy, P. Brisson, J.-L. Bost, J. Benda, R. Caillois, A. Camus, M. Fombeure, J. Guéhenno, H. Jeanson, J. Lescure, M. Leiris, J. Lemarchand, R. Maheu,

M. Merleau-Ponty, F. Mauriac, Brice-Parain, J. Paulhan, J.-P. Sartre, J. Schlumberger, P. Soupault.

36. See 'Le Cas Nizan', *Combat*, April 1947, reproduced in *Les Temps Modernes*, no. 22 (July 1947), pp. 181–4.
37. Ibid. 'M. Martin-Chauffier, in agreement with us on the substance of our protest, has not signed because he disapproves its tone and form.'
38. 'Mise au point du Comité National des Ecrivains', *Les Lettres françaises*, 11 April 1947; reproduced in *Les Temps Modernes*, no. 22 (July 1947), p. 182.
39. 'La Réponse de J.-P. Sartre au CNE', *Les Temps Modernes*, no. 22 (July 1947), p. 183.
40. Ibid. Lefebvre subsequently retracted the allegation in *La Somme et le reste* (La Nef de Pais, 1959).
41. Cited in C. Connolly, 'The Nizan Case', *Horizon*, June 1947, pp. 305–9.
42. Ibid.
43. P. Daix, in M. Contat and J. Lecarme, 'Les Années Sartre'.
44. Ibid.
45. A. Lecoeur, in 'Mémoires d'Ex', television film (Mosco) produced by Richard Copans for La Sept and broadcast on 19 and 23 January 1991.
46. J. Paulhan, *De la paille et le grain* (Gallimard, 1948); and *Lettre aux Directeurs de la Résistance* (Ramsay, 1987).
47. *Les Lettres françaises*, 22 November 1946; reproduced in J. Paulhan, *De la paille et le grain* (Gallimard, 1948), p. 95.
48. J. Paulhan, *Lettre aux Directeurs de la Résistance* (Editions Ramsay, 1987), pp. 35–49.
49. J. Pouillon, Letter to Michael Scriven, 25 August 1991.
50. Jean Paulhan refers approvingly to Sartre's revelations of Aragon's duplicitous attempts to dishonour Nizan in *De la paille et le grain* (Gallimard, 1948), p. 88.
51. J.-P. Sartre, *Préface à Aden Arabie* (François Maspero, 1960), p. 7.
52. P. McCarthey assesses Sartre's attitude to Nizan in the following terms: 'Paradoxically, Nizan is too much of a communist to please the 1948 Sartre and too much of an ex-communist to please the 1952 Sartre' – 'Sartre, Nizan and the Dilemmas of Commitment', in F. Jameson (ed.),

'Sartre after Sartre', *Yale Fench Studies*, no. 68 (New Haven, Conn.: Yale University Press, 1985), p. 200.

53. Both Walter Redfern and Pascal Ory argue that Nizan was the inspiration of the characters of Brunet and Schneider-Vicarios in *Les Chemins de la liberté*. See W. Redfern, *Paul Nizan: Committed Literature in a Conspiratorial World* (Princeton: Princeton University Press, 1972), pp. 206–9; and P. Ory, *Nizan: Destin d'un révolté* (Editions Ramsay, 1980), pp. 234–5.
54. J.-P. Sartre, 'Drôle d'amitié', in *Les Temps Modernes*, no. 49 (November 1949), pp. 769–806, and no. 50 (December 1949), pp. 1009–39; subsequently published in *Sartre Oeuvres romanesques* (Gallimard, 1981), pp. 1533–4.
55. A. Pierrard, in 'Mémoires d'Ex'.
56. See, for example, P. Nizan, *L'Humanité*, 29 September 1935.
57. A. Lecoeur, in 'Mémoires d'Ex'.
58. C. Morgan, *Les Don Quichotte et les autres* (Editions Roblot, 1972), p. 12.
59. SIT2, p. 329, n. 23.

5 SARTRE AND THE POLITICS OF VIOLENCE: MAOISM IN THE AFTERMATH OF MAY 1968

1. J.-P. Sartre, *Critique de la raison dialectique* (Gallimard, 1960), p. 209; English translation (London: New Left Books, 1976), p. 133.
2. Ibid., pp. 208–9; English translation, pp. 132–3.
3. It is worth registering Sartre's own interest in boxing when he was a young man. Unlike his intellectual peers of the time – for example Aron, who played tennis, Canguilhem and Lucot who played rugby, sports in which the prime attributes are either team-spirit or technical ability – Sartre preferred a sport based on aggressiveness and force in which the objective is to overwhelm the opponent physically. See A. Cohen-Solal, *Sartre 1905–1980* (Gallimard, 1985), p. 100.
4. J.-P. Sartre, *Critique de la raison dialectique (tome II)* (Gallimard, 1985), p. 45.

5. Ibid., p. 53.
6. 'Sartre parle des maos', interview with Michel-Antoine Burnier, *Actuel*, 28 February 1973, p. 76.
7. See also M. Scriven, 'Sartre and the Nizan Affair', *Sartre Studies International*, vol. 2, no. 1 (1996), pp. 19–39.
8. J. Cau, in M. Contat and J. Lecarme, 'Les Années Sartre', radio programme broadcast on France Culture, 24 and 25 August 1990.
9. J.-P. Sartre, Avant-propos aux *Maos en France* de Michèle Monceaux (Gallimard, 1972); reprinted in SIT10, p. 38.
10. SIT8, pp. 329–30.
11. J.-P. Sartre, Avant-propos aux *Maos en France*, p. 45.
12. J.-P. Sartre, *Critique de la raison dialectique* (Gallimard, 1960), p. 209; English translation pp. 132–3.
13. See in this respect F. Noudelmann, 'Sartre et l'inhumain', *Les Temps Modernes*, nos 565–6 (September 1993), pp. 48–65.
14. D. Rondeau, in B.-H. Lévy, 'les Aventures de la liberté', television programme broadcast on Antenne 2, March–April 1991. A striking example of the saintly, 'Robin Hood' character of Maoist terorism occurred in May 1970 when a group of Maoist militants raided the high-class store Fauchon, stole a variety of foodstuffs (caviar, foie gras), and subsequently redistributed them among the working-class inhabitants of Saint Denis. See H. Hamon and P. Rotman, *Génération* (Seuil, 1988), pp. 169–71.
15. Interview with Liliane Siegel, 3 September 1993.
16. S. de Beauvoir, *La Cérémonie des adieux* (Gallimard, 1981), p. 44.
17. C. Jambet, in B.-H. Lévy, 'Les Aventures de la liberté'.
18. J.-P. Sartre, Archives ORTF, 4 December 1974.
19. J.-P. Le Dantec, in F. Miterrand, 'Sartre, une vie', television programme broadcast on Antenne 2, 15 April 1990.
20. J.-P. Sartre, in B.-H. Lévy, 'Les Aventures de la liberté'.
21. 'States of Terror', television programme broadcast on Channel 4, November 1993.
22. Ibid.
23. Ibid.

24. For a detailed account of Sartre's involvement in the revolutionary press, see: (i) S. de Beauvoir, *Tout compte fait* (Gallimard, 1972), pp. 478–92, and *La Cérémonie des adieux* (Gallimard, 1981), pp. 15–25; (ii) M. Scriven, *Sartre and the Media* (London: Macmillan, 1993), pp. 60–9.
25. S. de Beauvoir, *Tout compte fait* (Gallimard, 1972), p. 478.
26. J.-P. Sartre, 'L'Alibi', *Le Nouvel observateur*, 19 November 1964; reprinted in SIT8, pp. 142–3.
27. See, for example, (i) J.-P Sartre, 'Deux poids, deux mesures', *La Cause du Peuple*, no. 26 (10 July 1969); (ii) J.-P. Sartre, 'Le Tournant de la fascisation: le tribunal populaire contre la police', *La Cause du Peuple-J'Accuse*, no. 6 (28 June 1971).
28. On 21 June 1972 Sartre instigated a debate on the nature and function of the revolutionary press in the columns of *La Cause du Peuple–J'Accuse*. See J.-P. Sartre, 'Ouverture d'un débat sur *La Cause du Peuple*', *La Cause du Peuple–J'Accuse*, no. 25 (21 June 1972).
29. 'Sartre parle des maos', interview with Michel-Antoine Burnier, *Actuel*, 28 February 1973, p. 74.
30. J.-P. Sartre, Avant-propos aux *Maos en France*, p. 39.

6 SARTRE AND COMMITMENT: REINVENTING CULTURAL FORMS

1. Jean-Paul Sartre, in M. Contat and J. Lecarme, 'Les Années Sartre', radio programme broadcast on France Culture 24 and 25 August 1990.
2. R. Debray, in M. Contat and J. Lecarme, 'Les Années Sartre', radio programme broadcast on France Culture 24 and 25 August 1990.
3. 'Radioscopie: *Roland Barthes*', interview with J. Chancel, 17 February 1975. Published in J. Chancel, *Radioscopie*, vol. 4 (Robert Laffont, 1976), pp. 255–6.
4. SIT2, p. 13.
5. See in this respect: M. Kelly, 'Humanism and National Unity: the Ideological Reconstruction of France', in N. Hewitt (ed.), *The Culture of Reconstruction: European*

Literature, Thought and Film, 1945–50 (London: Macmillan, 1989), pp. 103–19.

6. Madeleine Chapsal, *Les Ecrivains en Personne* (Editions Julliard, 1960), pp. 30–44.
7. J.-P. Sartre and M. Sicard, 'Entretien', *Sartre Inédit, Obliques*, 18–19 (1979), p. 28.
8. See M. Scriven, *Sartre's Existential Biographies* (London: Macmillan, 1984), pp. 29–44.
9. For a detailed account of Sartre's cultural activities during the Cold War period see M. Scriven, 'Cold War Polarization and Cultural Productivity in the Work of Sartre', *French Cultural Studies*, vol. 8, pt 1 (1997), pp. 117–26.
10. The last published part of *Les Chemins de la liberté, La Mort dans l'âme* appeared in 1949. Sartre's last play, *Les Séquestrés d'Altona*, was produced in 1959, although a Sartrean adaptation of Euripides's *Les Troyennes* appeared in 1965.
11. Awarded the Nobel Prize for literature following the publication of *Les Mots* in 1964, Sartre refused this prestigious accolade on the grounds that he did not wish to become the spokesperson of a Western bourgeois cultural institution. For an account of *Les Mots* as an example of existential biography, see M. Scriven, *Sartre's Existential Biographies* (London: Macmillan, 1984), pp. 94–103.
12. SIT10, pp. 61–2.

7 MYTH VERSUS SATIRE: THE DRAMATISED POLITICS OF SARTRE'S *NEKRASSOV*

1. Henry Magnan, 'Avant la création de *Nekrassov* au Théâtre Antoine, Sartre nous dit…', *Le Monde*, 1 June 1955, p. 9.
2. *Nekrassov*, Sartre's ninth play, was performed for the first time at the Théâtre Antoine in Paris on 8 June 1955, and ran for 60 performances. It was subsequently produced in 1968 at the Théâtre de Strasbourg, and again in 1978 at the Théâtre de l'Est in Paris. The first

performance of the play in English was in 1957 at the Unity Theatre in London. The text of the play was originally published in extracts in *Les Temps Modernes*, nos 114–15 (June–July 1955), pp. 2017–71; no. 116 (August 1955), pp. 85–125; no. 117 (September 1955), pp. 277–323 and an edition was published by Gallimard in 1956. An additional scene, cut from the original production and entitled 'Le Bal des Futurs Fusillés', was published in *Les Lettres françaises*, 16–23 June 1955, and subsequently reprinted in ES, pp. 714–19. An English translation by Sylvia and George Leeson was published by Hamish Hamilton in 1957.

3. Anon., 'Explosions au Théâtre Antoine à propos de la pièce "crypto" de Jean-Paul Sartre', *Le Figaro*, 10 May 1955, p. 10.
4. See: (i) Jean-Jacques Gautier, 'Au Théâtre Antoine *Nekrassov* de Jean-Paul Sartre', *Le Figaro*, 13 June 1955, p. 12; (ii) Thierry Maulnier, 'L'Opium du peuple', *Le Figaro*, 4 July 1955, p. 1.
5. Robert Kemp, '*Nekrassov* au Théâtre Antoine', *Le Monde*, 14 June 1955, p. 11.
6. Ibid.
7. It was alleged in right-wing circles that Sartre had expressly written *Nekrassov* in order to atone for the 'anti-communist' thesis of *Les Mains sales*, performed for the first time on 2 April 1948. The extent of communist hostility to *Les Mains sales* can be gauged from the following reaction to the play cited by Simone de Beauvoir in *La Force des choses* (Gallimard, 1963), p. 168: 'For thirty pieces of silver and a mess of American potage, M. J.-P. Sartre has sold his last remaining vestiges of honour and probity'.
8. Guy Leclerc, 'Au Théâtre Antoine: *Nekrassov* de Jean-Paul Sartre', *L'Humanité*, 13 June 1955, p. 2.
9. Pierre Daix, '*Nekrassov* ou le défi de la critique au public', *Les Lettres françaises*, 23 June 1955, p. 2.
10. (i) Claude-Henry Leconte, 'La dure bataille de *Nekrassov* laisse intact le moral de la troupe', *Combat*, 2 June 1955, p. 2; (ii) Serge Montigny, 'A la veille de la première de

Nekrassov: Jean-Paul Sartre', *Combat*, 7 June 1955, pp. 1–2.

11. Anon., 'Lecture de *Nekrassov*', *Combat*, 13 July 1955, p. 2.
12. Thierry Maulnier, '*Nekrassov* au Théâtre Antoine', *Combat*, 13 June 1955, p. 2.
13. André Alter, '*Nekrassov*: Un pétard mouillé de Jean-Paul Sartre', *Témoignage chrétien*, 24 June 1955. It is worth recording that Gabriel Marcel, while highlighting the 'dangerous' political implications of *Nekrassov*, judged it to be a superior theatrical experience to *Le Diable et le bon dieu* ('*Nekrassov* par Jean-Paul Sartre', *Les Nouvelles littéraires*, 16 June 1955). Marcel's preference for *Nekrassov* can doubtless be explained as the product of Catholic hostility to the 'moral' thesis of *Le Diable et le bon dieu*.
14. Roland Barthes, '*Nekrassov* juge de sa critique', *Théâtre populaire*, no. 14 (July–August 1955).
15. See, for example: (a) Richard Findlater, 'First-Class Theatre – Third-Class Politics', *Tribune*, 13 January 1956, p. 8; (b) Ted Gomm, 'A Socialist at the Theatre', *Socialist Leader*, vol. 44, no. 40 (5 October 1956), p. 2; (c) William Salter, 'Murrow, Thomas, Sartre', *The New Statesman and Nation*, 1 September 1956, pp. 241–2; (d) T. C. Worsley, 'The Arts and Entertainment: A Political Farce', *The New Statesman and Nation*, 14 January 1956, pp. 40–1.
16. Ossia Trilling, '*Nekrassov* by Jean-Paul Sartre', *London Magazine*, vol. 4, no 7 (1957), pp. 75–9.
17. Jean-Paul Sartre, *Les Communistes ont peur de la révolution* (Editions John Didier, 1969).
18. See (a) Robert Abirached, 'Jean-Paul Sartre: *Nekrassov*, par le Théâtre National de Strasbourg', *La Nouvelle Revue Française*, 33 (1969), pp. 313–14; (b) Jean Besse, '*Nekrassov* réhabilité', *Les Lettres françaises*, November– December 1968, pp. 26–7; (c) B. Poiret-Delpech, '*Nekrassov* de Jean-Paul Sartre', *Le Monde*, 13 November 1968, p. 25.
19. See (a) Jean-Marie Borzeix, 'La Bataille de *Nekrassov* n'aura pas lieu, hélas!', *Les Nouvelles Littéraires*, 9 February 1978, p. 3; (b) Gilles Sandier, 'La reprise de *Nekrassov*', *La Quinzaine littéraire*, 16 March 1978, p. 21;

(c) Philippe Sénart, '*Nekrassov* (Théâtre de l'Est parisien)', *Revue des deux Mondes*, April–June 1978, pp. 188–90; (d) Bruno Villien, '*Nekrassov*, vingt ans après', *Le Nouvel observateur*, 27 February–5 March 1978, pp. 86–7.

20. 'Entretien avec Kenneth Tynan', in TDS, pp. 158–9.
21. For an excellent discussion of the differences between Sartrean and Brechtian theatre, see (i) J.-P Sartre, 'Théâtre épique et théâtre dramatique', TDS, pp. 104–51: (ii) '*Les Séquestrés d'Altona* nous concernent tous', interview with Bernard Dort, *Théâtre populaire*, no 36, 1959, reprinted in TDS, pp. 299–314.
22. Guy Leclerc, '"En dénonçant dans ma nouvelle pièce les procédés de la presse anticommuniste, je veux apporter une contribution d'écrivain à la lutte pour la paix" nous déclare Jean-Paul Sartre', *L'Humanité*, 8 June 1955, p. 2.
23. See ibid.
24. Ibid.
25. For an account of Sartre's transitional status as a writer in postwar France, see M. Scriven, *Sartre's Existential Biographies* (London: Macmillan, 1984).
26. Leclerc, 'En dénonçant dans ma nouvelle pièce ...'.
27. 'Tableau inédit de *Nekrassov*: le Bal des Futurs Fusillés', *Les Lettres françaises*, 16–23 June 1955. In this scene, Jean-Jacques Gautier is cited by name, Champenois bears a marked resemblance to Georges Altman, and Cocardeau to André Malraux.
28. Jean-Paul Sartre, *L'Imaginaire* (Gallimard, 1940), p. 371.
29. Ibid.
30. Thierry Maulnier, 'L'Opium du peuple', *Le Figaro*, 4 July 1955, p. 1.
31. Thierry Maulnier, 'Nékroutchov?', *Le Figaro*, 18 July 1956, p. 2.
32. Gabriel Marcel, '*Nekrassov* par Jean-Paul Sartre', *Les Nouvelles Littéraires*, 16 June 1955, p. 6.
33. J.-F Rolland, 'Jean-Paul Sartre vous parle de *Nekrassov*: La pièce vise les institutions et non des individus', *L'Humanité*, 19 June 1955.
34. ES, p. 283.
35. Annie Cohen-Solal, *Sartre* (Gallimard, 1985), p. 461.

36. Henry Magnan, 'Avant la création de *Nekrassov* au Théâtre Antoine, Sartre nous dit…', *Le Monde*, 1 June 1955, p. 9.
37. 'Entretien avec Kenneth Tynan', in TDS, p. 159.

8 IDEOLOGICAL ART CRITICISM: SARTRE AND GIACOMETTI

1. 'Paris Post War: Art and Existentialism 1945–55', Tate Gallery, London, 9 June–5 September 1993. The catalogue of the exhibition, F. Morris, *Paris Post War: Art and Existentialism 1945–55* (London: Tate Gallery, 1993), contains two extensively documented contextualising essays: (i) S. Wilson, 'Paris Post War; In Search of the Absolute', pp. 25–52; (ii) D. Mellor, 'Existentialism and Post War British Art', pp. 53–62. A version of this chapter on Sartre and Giacometti was originally delivered as a lecture at the Tate Gallery on 10 July 1993 as a contribution to the educational events linked to the exhibition.
2. D. Sylvester, 'In Giacometti's Studio', *Independent*, 10 July 1993, p. 29. For a broader assessment of the exhibition, see C. Howells, 'A new resolve: Art and existentialism in the wake of the Second World War', *The Times Literary Supplement*, 2 July 1993, pp. 18–19.
3. J.-P. Sartre, 'La Recherche de l'absolu', *Les Temps Modernes*, no. 28 (January 1948), pp. 1153–63; reprinted in SIT3, pp. 289–305. The text, translated as 'The Search for the Absolute', constituted the introducton to the catalogue of an exhibition of Giacometti's sculptures at the Pierre Matisse Gallery in New York, 10 January–14 February 1948.
4. J.-P. Sartre, 'Les Peintures de Giacometti', *Derrière le miroir* (Review of the Maeght Gallery), no. 65 (May 1954); reprinted in *Les Temps Modernes*, no. 103 (June 1954), pp. 2221–32 and in SIT4, pp. 347–63. The text constituted the introduction to the catalogue of an exhibition of Giacometti's paintings at the Maeght Gallery, 14 May–15 June 1954.

5. *Wols en personne*, Jean-Paul Sartre, Henri-Pierre Roche and Werner Hauftmann (Delpire, 1962); the text by Sartre was reprinted as 'Doigts et non-doigts', in SIT4, pp. 408–34.
6. SIT2, p. 63; SIT4, p. 368.
7. J.-P. Sartre, 'Mythe et réalité du théâtre', *Le Point*, no. 7 (January 1967), pp. 20–5.
8. 'Paris Post War: Matter and Memory', conference held at the Tate Gallery, 18 June 1993. Speakers were: Tim Mathews ('Fautrier: Image and Body'), Sarah Wilson ('Sartre and Art: From Surrealism to Existentialism'), Raymond Mason ('School of Paris'), Alphons Grieder ('Visions of Man: Phenomenological, Existential and Giacomettian'), Michael Kelly ('Deaths and Entrances: Ideas and Ideology in Post War France'), Elsa Adamowicz ('Michaux: Making Faces'), Patrick Marsh ('Resnais: Film and Memory'), and Michel Oriano, William Turnbull, Olivier Todd, Bryan Robertson ('Round Table Discussion').
9. Sarah Wilson, 'Sartre and Art', n. 8.
10. Ibid.
11. Raymond Mason, 'School of Paris', n. 8.
12. Alphons Grieder, 'Visions of Man', n. 8.
13. Olivier Todd; n. 8.
14. J. Cau, in M. Contat and J. Lecarme, 'Les Années Sartre', radio programme broadcast on France Culture, 24 and 25 August 1990.
15. J.-P. Sartre, 'Réponse à Albert Camus', *Les Temps Modernes*, no. 82 (August 1952), pp. 334–53; reprinted in SIT4, pp. 90–129.
16. J.-P. Sartre, 'La Réponse de Jean-Paul Sartre au CNE', *Les Temps Modernes*, no. 22 (July 1947), pp. 181–4.
17. J.-P. Sartre, 'M. François Mauriac et la liberté', *La Nouvelle Revue Française*, no. 305 (February 1939), pp. 212–32; reprinted in SIT1, pp. 35–52.
18. J.-P. Sartre, 'Les Bastilles de Raymond Aron', *Le Nouvel Observateur*, 19–25 June 1968; reprinted in SIT8, pp. 193–207.

19. The emergence of existentialism as the 'cultural glue' of postwar intellectual practice was assessed in detail by Michael Kelly at the Tate Gallery conference; see n. 8. See also M. Kelly, 'Humanism and National Unity: the Ideological Reconstruction of France', in N. Hewitt (ed.), *The Culture of Reconstruction: European Literaure, Thought and Film, 1945–50* (London: Macmillan, 1989), pp. 103–19.
20. R. Barthes, 'Qu'est-ce que la critique ?', in *Essais critiques* (Seuil, 1964), pp. 252–7.
21. For an account of this process of ideological criticism in Sartre's work, see M. Scriven, *Sartre's Existential Biographies* (London: Macmillan, 1984).
22. J.-P. Sartre, *Saint Genet, comédien et martyr* (Gallimard, 1952). Genet himself wrote a perceptive analysis of Giacometti's work: 'L'Atelier d'Alberto Giacometti', *Les Lettres Nouvelles*, vol. 5, no. 52. (September 1957), pp. 199–218; reprinted in *Jean Genet Oeuvres Complètes* (Gallimard, 1979), pp. 39–73.
23. For a comprehensive account of Sartre's approach to the visual arts, see (i) G. Bauer, *Sartre and the Artist* (Chicago: Chicago University Press, 1969); (ii) M. Sicard, 'Esthétique de Sartre', *Obliques Sartre et les Arts* (1981), pp. 15–20.
24. J.-P. Sartre and M. Sicard, 'Penser l'art: entretien', *Obliques Sartre et les Arts* (1981), pp. 15–20.
25. J.-P. Sartre, *La Nausée* (Gallimard, 1938), pp. 120, 129 and 135–6. It is worth comparing the Bouville museum incident in *La Nausée* with the short piece that Sartre wrote entited 'Portraits officiels', *Verve*, nos 5–6 (1939), pp. 9–12; reprinted in ES, pp. 557–9.
26. J.-P. Sartre, 'Le séquestré de Venise', *Les Temps Modernes*, no. 141 (November 1957), pp. 761–800, reprinted in SIT4, pp. 291–346; J.-P. Sartre, 'Saint Georges et le dragon', *L'Arc*, no. 30 (October 1966), pp. 35–50, reprinted in SIT9, pp. 202–26; J.-P. Sartre, 'Saint Marc et son double', *Obliques: Sartre et les Arts* (1981), pp. 171–202.

27. J.-P. Sartre, 'Visages', *Verve*, nos 5–6, pp. 43–4; reprinted in ES, pp. 560–4.
28. J.-P. Sartre, *Visages, précédé de Portraits officiels* (Seghers, 1948).
29. J.-P. Sartre, 'Visages', p. 564.
30. Ibid., p. 560.
31. J.-P. Sartre, *Les Mots* (Gallimard, 1964), p. 193.
32. S. de Beauvoir, *La Force de l'âge* (Gallimard, 1960), p. 561.
33. Ibid.
34. Ibid., pp. 561–2.
35. J.-P. Sartre, *Les Mots* (Gallimard, 1964), pp. 193–4.
36. Ibid., pp. 194–5.
37. S. de Beauvoir, *Tout compte fait* (Gallimard, 1972), p. 102.
38. SIT3, pp. 292–3.
39. Ibid., p. 294.
40. J.-P. Sartre, *L'Imaginaire* (Gallimard, 1940).
41. S. de Beauvoir, *Tout compte fait* (Gallimard, 1972), p. 103.
42. 'Rétrospective Alberto Giacometti', exhibition held at the Musée d'Art Moderne, Paris, 30 November 1991–15 March 1992.
43. J.-P. Sartre and M. Sicard, 'Penser l'art: entretien', *Obliques Sartre et les Arts* (1981), p. 16.

9 MEDIATED POLITICS: SARTRE AND CHOMSKY REVISITED

1. An extended version of this chapter was delivered as my inaugural professorial lecture at the University of Bath on 3 May 1994.
2. M. Contat and M. Rybalka, 'Un Entretien avec J.-P. Sartre', *Le Monde des livres*, 14 May 1971.
3. E. Balladur, 'Interview Pompidou', *Le Point*, 19 March 1994, p. 36.
4. 'Manufacturing Consent – Noam Chomsky and the Media; Thought Control in a Democratic Society', Canadian-made film produced by M. Achbar and P. Wintonick broadcast on Channel 4 'Channels of Resistance' series, 1993.

5. 'Berlusconi win could halt "virtuous circle"', *The Times Higher Education Supplement*, 8 April 1994, p. 6.
6. S. de Beauvoir, *La Force des choses* (Gallimard, 1963), p. 33.
7. SIT4, p. 100.
8. *Libération*, special number, 5 February 1973.
9. SIT10, p. 220.
10. J.-P. Sartre, 'L'Ami du peuple', *L'Idiot international*, no. 10 (September 1970), p. 35; reprinted in SIT8, pp. 456–76.
11. P. Hervé, 'Sophie a des malheurs', *Action*, 5 November 1947, p. 2.
12. Cited by Michel Contat during a radio programme broadcast by France Culture on 25 August 1989 entitled 'L'Avenir de la France'. The programme was centred on the contemporary significance of the 'Tribune des *Temps Modernes*'.
13. 'Radioscopie: Jean-Paul Sartre', interview with J. Chancel, 7 February 1973. Published in J. Chancel, *Radioscopie*, vol. 1 (Robert Laffont, 1973), pp. 187–215.
14. *Le Monde*, 23 September 1972.
15. J.-P. Sartre, interview with Olivier Todd, 'Le Massacre de Song My', Panorama, Première Chaîne ORTF, 11 December 1969. See (i) J.-P. Sartre, 'On tue les Vietnamiens parce qu'ils sont vietnamiens', *Voix ouvrière*, 13 December 1969; (ii) C. Durieux, 'M. J.-P. Sartre et le massacre de Song My au magazine Panorama', *Le Monde*, 13 December 1969, p. 15.
16. Ibid.
17. See: S. de Beauvoir, *La Cérémonie des adieux* (Gallimard, 1981), p. 158.
18. G. Orwell, preface to envisaged private publication of *Animal Farm*; see P. Lewis, *George Orwell: The Road to 1984* (London: Heinemann, 1981), p. 97.
19. N. Chomsky, 'Thought Control in a Democratic Society'.
20. J.-P. Sartre, 'Des rats et des hommes', préface au *Traître* d'André Gorz; reprinted in SIT4, pp. 38–81.

POSTCRIPT

1. B. Lévy, in M. Contat and J. Lecarme, 'Les Années Sartre', radio programme broadcast on France Culture 24 and 25 August 1990.
2. SIT8, pp. 186–7.

Bibliography

The bibliography is in three parts. The first and second parts constitute the primary and secondary sources relevant to those aspects of Sartre's political and cultural evolution analysed in the preceding pages. The third part comprises a list of theoretical, methodological and ideological texts which have been instrumental in the formulation of the specific critical viewpoint adopted in this book. For a more comprehensive account of Sartre's work and Sartre criticism in general, the reader is referred to the following texts which contain extensive bibliographical references.

Contat, M. and M. Rybalka, *Les Ecrits de Sartre: Chronologie Bibliographie commentée* (Gallimard, 1970); trans. Richard C. McCleary, *The Writings of Jean-Paul Sartre* (Evanston, Ill.: North Western University Press, 1974).

——, 'Les Ecrits de Sartre de 1969 à 1971', *Le Magazine Littéraire*, no. 55–6 (September 1971), pp. 36–47.

——, 'Les Ecrits de Sartre (1973–1978)', *Obliques*, no. 18 (1979), pp. 335–44.

——, *Sartre: Bibliographie 1980–1992* (CNRS Editions, 1993).

Lapointe, F.H., *Jean-Paul Sartre and his Critics: An International Bibliography (1938–80)*, annotated and rev. 2nd edn (Bowling Green, OH: Philosophy Documentation Center, 1981).

Wilcocks, R., *Jean-Paul Sartre: A Bibliography of International Criticism* (Edmonton: University of Alberta Press, 1975).

POLITICS AND HISTORY

Primary Sources

Sartre, J.-P., D. Rousset and G. Rosenthal, *Entretiens sur la politique* (Gallimard, 1949).

Sartre, J.-P., *Situations V, colonialisme et néo-colonialisme* (Gallimard, 1964).

Sartre, J.-P., *Situations VI, problèmes du marxisme 1* (Gallimard, 1964).

Sartre, J.-P., *Situations VII, problèmes du marxisme 2* (Gallimard, 1965).
Sartre, J.-P., *Situations VIII, autour de 68* (Gallimard, 1972).
Sartre, J.-P., *Situations X, politique et autobiographie* (Gallimard, 1976).
Sartre, J.-P., *Les Communistes ont peur de la révolution* (Editions John Didier, 1969).
Sartre, J.-P., P. Gavi and B. Victor, *On a raison de se révolter* (Gallimard, 1974).

For a detailed bibliography of Sartre's political contributions to the press, radio and television broadcasting, see: M. Scriven, *Sartre and the Media* (London: Macmillan, 1993), pp. 138–46.

Secondary Sources

Aron, R., *Mémoires* (Julliard, 1983).
Aronson, R. and A. Dobson, 'Discussion of "Sartre and Stalin"', *Sartre Studies International*, vol. 3, no. 1 (1997), pp. 16–21.
Barilier, E., *Les Petits camarades: essai sur Jean-Paul Sartre et Raymond Aron* (Julliard/l'Age d'Homme, 1987).
Beauvoir, S. de, *La Cérémonie des adieux* (Gallimard, 1981).
——, *La Force des choses* (Gallimard, 1963).
——, *Journal de guerre* (Gallimard, 1990).
——, *Lettres a Sartre: 1940–1963* (Gallimard, 1990).
——, *Tout compte fait* (Gallimard, 1972).
Birchall, I., 'Sartre's Encounter with Daniel Guérin', *Sartre Studies International*, vol. 2, no. 1 (1996), pp. 41–56.
Boschetti, A., *Sartre et Les Temps Modernes* (Minuit, 1985).
Burnier, M.-A., *Les Existentialistes et la politique* (Gallimard, 1966).
——, *Le Testament de Sartre* (Olivier Orban, 1982).
Cau, J., 'Sartre', in *Croquis de mémoire* (Julliard, 1985), pp. 229–59.
Caute, D., *Communism and the French Intellectuals: 1914–1960* (London: André Deutsch, 1964).
——, *The Fellow Travellers* (London: Quartet, 1977).
Chebel d'Appollonia, A., *Histoire politique des intellectuels en France, 1945–1954* (Editions Complexe, 1991).
Cohen-Solal, A., *Sartre: 1905–1980* (Gallimard, 1985).

Contat, M., 'Was Sartre a Democrat?', *Sartre Studies International*, vol. 2, no. 1 (1996), pp. 1–17.

Dantec, J.-P. Le, *Les Dangers du soleil* (Les Presses d'aujourd'hui, 1978).

Davies, H., *Sartre and Les Temps Modernes* (Cambridge: Cambridge University Press, 1987).

Dobson, A., *Jean-Paul Sartre and the Politics of Reason* (Cambridge: Cambridge Univesity Press, 1993).

——, 'Sartre and Stalin: *Critique of Dialectical Reason*, vol. 2', *Sartre Studies International*, vol. 3, no. 1 (1997), pp. 1–15.

Drake, D., 'Sartre and May 1968: The Intellectual in Crisis', *Sartre Studies International*, vol. 3, no. 1 (1997), pp. 43–65.

Fe, F., *Sartre e il communismo* (Firenze: La Nuova Italia, 1970).

Gerassi, J., *Jean-Paul Sartre. Hated Consciousness of His Century, Vol. 1: Protestant or Protestor?* (Chicago: University of Chicago Press, 1989).

Hamon, H. and P. Rotman, *Génération* (Seuil, 1988).

Hervé, P., *La Révolution et les fétiches* (La Table Ronde, 1956).

——, *Lettre a Sartre* (La Table Ronde, 1956).

Jeanson, F., *Sartre dans sa vie* (Seuil, 1974).

Joseph, G., *Une si douce occupation: Simone de Beauvoir et Jean-Paul Sartre 1940–1944* (Albin Michel, 1991).

Lévy, B.-H., *Les Aventures de la liberté: une histoire subjective des intellectuels* (Grasset, 1991).

McBride, W., *Sartre's Political Theory* (Bloomington and Indianapolis: Indiana University Press, 1991).

Naville, P., 'Les Mésaventures de Nekrassov', *France-Observateur*, 8 March 1956.

Reader, K., *Intellectuals and the Left in France since 1968* (London: Macmillan, 1987).

Sauvageot, J., A. Geismar, D. Cohn-Bendit, and J.-P. Duteil, *La Révolte étudiante* (Seuil, 1968).

Scriven, M., *Paul Nizan, Communist Novelist* (London: Macmillan, 1988).

——, 'Sartre and the Nizan Affair', *Sartre Studies International*, vol. 2, no. 1 (1996), pp. 19–39.

——, *Sartre and the Media* (London: Macmillan, 1993).

——, 'Sartre attiré et repoussé par la télévision', *Les Temps Modernes*, nos 531–33 (1990), pp. 1072–95.

——, 'Television Images of Sartre', *French Cultural Studies*, vol. 3, pt 1 (1992), pp. 87–92.
Siegel, L., *La Clandestine* (Maren Sell, 1988)
Sirinelli, J.-F., *Intellectuels et passions françaises: manifestes et pétitions au vingtième siècle* (Fayard, 1990).
Steiner, G., 'Sartre: The Suspect Witness', *The Times Literary Supplement*, 3 May 1991, pp. 3–5.
Todd, O., *Albert Camus, une vie* (Gallimard, 1996).
——, *Un fils rebelle* (Grasset, 1981).

CULTURE

Primary Sources

Sartre, J.-P., *Situations I, essais critiques* (Gallimard, 1947).
Sartre, J.-P., *Situations II, Qu'est-ce que la littérature?* (Gallimard, 1948).
Sartre, J.-P., *Situations III* (Gallimard, 1949).
Sartre, J-P., *Situations IV, portraits* (Gallimard, 1964).
Sartre, J.-P., *Situations IX, mélanges* (Gallimard, 1972).
Sartre, J.-P., *Un théâtre de situations* (Gallimard, 1973).
Sartre, J.-P., *Nekrassov* (Gallimard, 1956).

Secondary Sources

Aronson, R., *Jean-Paul Sartre: Philosophy in the World* (London: New Left Books, 1980).
——, 'Sartre and Marxism: A Double Retrospective', *Sartre Studies International*, vol. 1, nos 1/2 (1995), pp. 21–36.
Barnes, H., *Sartre* (London: Quartet, 1973).
——, *Sartre and Flaubert* (Chicago: University of Chicago Press, 1981).
——, *The Literature of Possibility; A Study in Humanistic Existentialism* (London: Tavistock Publications, 1961).
Bauer, G., *Sartre and the Artist* (Chicago: University of Chicago Press, 1969).
Caute, D., 'Sartre 1: Roads to Freedom', *New Statesman*, 2 May 1980, pp. 667–8.

——, 'Sartre 2: What is Literature?', *New Statesman*, 9 May 1980, pp. 716–17.

——, 'Sartre 3: Force, of Circumstances', *New Statesman*, 16 May 1980, pp. 752–3.

——, 'Sartre 4: The Good and the Great', *New Statesman*, 22 May 1980, pp. 785–6.

——, 'Sartre's What is Literature?', *Collisions, Essays and Reviews* (London: Quartet, 1974), pp. 159–72.

Collins, D., *Sartre as Biographer* (Cambridge, Mass. and London: Harvard University Press, 1980).

Craib, I., *Existentialism and Sociology: A Study of Jean-Paul Sartre* (Cambridge: Cambridge University Press, 1976).

Cranston, M., *Sartre* (Edinburgh and London: Oliver & Boyd, 1962).

Desan, W., *The Marxism of Jean-Paul Sartre* (New York: Anchor, 1965).

Fell, J.P., *Emotion in the Thought of Sartre* (New York and London: Columbia University Press, 1965).

Flower, J., *Literature and the Left in France* (London: Macmillan, 1983).

Forbes, J. and M. Kelly (eds), *French Cultural Studies* (Oxford: Oxford University Press, 1995).

Garaudy, R., *Literature of the Graveyard* (New York: International Publishers, 1948).

Goldthorpe, R., *Sartre: Literature and Theory* (Cambridge: Cambridge University Press, 1987).

Halpern, J., *Critical Fictions, the Literary Criticism of Jean-Paul Sartre* (New Haven and London: Yale University Press, 1976).

Hewitt, N. (ed.), *The Culture of Reconstruction: European Literature, Thought and Film, 1945–50* (London: Macmillan, 1989).

Hill, C.G., *Jean-Paul Sartre: Freedom and Commitment* (New York: Peter Lang, 1992).

Howells, C., *Sartre's Theory of Literature* (London: Modern Humanities Reserach Association, 1976).

——, *Sartre: The Necessity of Freedom* (Cambridge: Cambridge University Press, 1988).

Jameson, F., *Sartre: The Origins of a Style* (New Haven and London: Yale University Press, 1961).

——, 'The Sartrean Origin', *Sartre Studies International*, vol. 1, nos 1/2 (1995), pp. 1–20.

Jeanson, F., *Le problème moral et la pensée de Sartre* (Seuil, 1965).

——, *Sartre par lui-même* (Seuil, 1955).

Keefe, T. and E. Smyth (eds), *Autobiography and the Existential Self* (Liverpool: Liverpool University Press, 1995).

La Capra, D., *A Preface to Sartre* (New York: Cornell University Press, 1978).

Laing, R.D. and D.G. Cooper, *Reason and Violence: A Decade in Sartre's Philosophy* (London: Tavistock Publications, 1964).

Lawler, J., *The Existentialist Marxism of Jean-Paul Sartre* (Atlantic Highlands, NJ: Humanities Press, 1976).

Leak, A., *The Perverted Consciousness. Sexuality and Sartre* (London: Macmillan, 1989).

——, 'Writing and Seduction I', *Sartre Studies International*, vol. 1, nos 1/2 (1995), pp. 57–75.

——, 'Writing and Seduction II', *Sartre Studies International*, vol. 2, no. 1 (1996), pp. 57–75.

Louette, J.-F., *Silences de Sartre* (Presses Universitaires du Mirail, 1995).

——, *Sartre contra Nietzsche* (Presses Universitaires de Grenoble, 1996).

Majumdar, M., 'The Intransigence of the Intellectual: Autonomy and Ideology in Althusser and Sartre', *Sartre Studies International*, vol. 3, no. 1 (1997), pp. 22–42.

Mészáros, I., *The Work of Sartre*, vol. I (Brighton: Harvester, 1979).

Murdoch, I., *Sartre, Romantic Rationalist* (London: Bowes & Bowes, 1953).

Pacaly, J., *Sartre au miroir* (Kliencksieck, 1980).

Poster, M., *Existential Marxism in Post-war France: from Sartre to Althusser* (Princeton, NJ: Princeton University Press, 1975).

——, *Sartre's Marxism* (London: Pluto Press, 1979).

Schalk, D.L., *The Spectrum of Political Engagement* (Princeton, NJ: Princeton University Press, 1979).

Scriven, M., *Sartre's Existential Biographies* (London: Macmillan, 1984).

——, 'Cold War Polarization and Cultural Productivity in the Work of Sartre', *French Cultural Studies*, vol. 8, pt 1, (1997), pp. 117–26.

——, '*L'Etre et le néant* 50 years on', *French Cultural Studies*, vol. 5, pt 1 (1994), pp. 105–7.
——, 'Press Exposure in Sartre's *Nekrassov*', *Journal of European Studies*, vol. 18 (1988), pp. 267–80.
——, 'Pour un théâtre de dénonciation', *Europe*, nos 784–5 (1994), pp. 109–21.
Sicard, M., *La Critique littéraire de J.-P. Sartre* (Minard, 1976).
Suhl, B., *Jean-Paul Sartre, the Philosopher as a Literary Critic* (New York and London: Columbia University Press, 1970).
Taylor, J. 'Psychasthenia in *La Nausée*', *Sartre Studies International*, vol. 1, nos 1/2 (1965), pp. 77–93.
Thody, P., *Jean-Paul Sartre, a Literary and Political Study* (London: Hamish Hamilton, 1960).

CRITICAL THEORY AND METHODOLOGY

Aron, R., *Marxismes imaginaires* (Gallimard, 1970).
Barthes, R., *Critique et vérité* (Seuil, 1966).
——, *Le Degré zéro de l'écriture* (Seuil, 1953).
——, *Essais critiques* (Seuil, 1964).
——, *Mythologies* (Seuil, 1957).
Bon, F., Burnier, M.-A., *Les Nouveaux intellectuels* (Seuil, 1966).
Caute, D.,*The Illusion: An Essay on Politics, Theatre and the Novel* (London: André Deutsch, 1971).
Chomsky, N., *Manufacturing Consent: Noam Chomsky and the Media* (Montreal and London: Black Rose, 1994).
Debray, R., *Le Pouvoir intellectuel en France* (Ramsay, 1979).
——, *Le Scribe* (Grasset, 1980)
Doubrovsky, S., *Pourquoi une nouvelle critique: critique et objectivité* (Mercure de France, 1966)
Eagleton, T., *Criticism and Ideology; A Study in Marxist Literary Theory* (London: Verso, 1978).
——,*The Function of Criticism* (London: Verso, 1984).
Goldmann, L., *La Création culturelle dans la société moderne* (Denoel Gonthier, 1971).
——, *Pour une sociologie du roman* (Gallimard, 1964).
——, *Sciences humaines et philosophie* (Gonthier, 1966).

——, *Structures mentales et création culturelle* (Anthropos, 1970).
Jameson, F., *Marxism and Form: Twentieth-century Dialectical Theories of Literature* (Princeton, NJ: Princeton University Press, 1974).
Lévi-Strauss, C., *La Pensée sauvage* (Plon, 1962).
Lukács, G., *Existentialisme ou marxisme?* (Plon, 1962).
——, *The Meaning of Contemporary Realism* (London: Merlin Press, 1963).
——, *Writer and Critic* (London: Merlin Press, 1978).
Merleau-Ponty, M., *Les Aventures de la dialectique* (Gallimard, 1955).
Nizan, P., *Aden-Arabie*, préface de J.-P. Sartre (Maspero, 1960).
——, *Les Chiens de garde* (Maspero, 1960).
Williams, R., *Culture and Society, 1780–1950* (London: Chatto & Windus, 1958).
——, *The Long Revolution* (London: Chatto & Windus, 1961).
——, *Marxism and Literature* (Oxford: Oxford University Press, 1977).

Index

Note: the most important discussions of a topic are indicated by page numbers in **bold** type.

Aden Arabie 42, 45, 55, 59, 93, 94
Affaire Henri Martin, L' 91
Age de raison, L' 91
Algeria 11, 14, 26, 28, 29, 66
Antenne 2 34, 35, 138, 147
Aragon, L. 48, 50, 53, 54, 55, 56, 116
Aristophanes 102
Aron, R. 25, 31, 32, 42, 45, 139, 140, 144
Artaud, A. 113
'articles agissants' 89
Aujourd'hui 54

Baader, A. 36, 73, 74
Balladur, E. 135
Bariona 101
Barthes, R. 85, 99, 117
'Bastilles de Raymond Aron, Les' 25
Baudelaire, C. 58
Baudelaire 91
Beauvoir, S. de 25, 43, 121, 122, 124, 125, 131, 139
Beaux enfants qui n'hésitez pas 48
Bénouville, G. de 25, 32, 144
Berlusconi, S. 138
Bonafé, A. 25
boxing 64, 65
Breton, A. 54
Burnier, M.-A. 65

Camus, A. 42, 115, 116, 139
Casanova, L. 50, 51, 54
Castro, F. 141
Cau, J. 45, 46, 66, 116
Cause du Peuple, La 33, 67, 72, 73, 75, 76, 77, 94, 95
Cause du Peuple–J'Accuse, La 67, 75, 77, 140
Cérémonie de adieux, La 72
'Ces années-là' 37
Chancel, J. 145
Chateaubriant, A. de 54
Chemins de la liberté, Les 44
Chiens de garde, Les 45
Chirac, J. 34, 35, 38, 139, 146, 147
Chomsky, N. 3, **133–51**
Clandestine, La 42
Claudel, P. 85
Clavel, M. 35
Cohn-Bendit, D. 31, 36
Cold War 12, 13, 14, 15, 18, 28, 43, 50, 51, 52, 54, 57, 58, 61, 91, 92, 97, 98, 102, 103, 107, 112, 116, 140, 141, 144
Collaboration 57
Combat 23, 98, 139
Cominform 50, 52, 57
Comité National des Ecrivains (CNE) 49, 50, 53, 57
commitment 3, 11, 58, 83–95
Commune 87
communism 3, 23, 43, 47, 92, 97, 103
Communistes, Les 48
'Communistes et la paix, Les' 14, 68, 91
'Communistes ont peur de la révolution, Les' 15
Communist International, The 56
Contat, M. xiii, 41, 42, 43
Critique de la raison dialectique 63, 64, 70, 91, 93
Croissant, K. 36
Cuba 14, 29, 66, 93, 94, 140, 141, 142
cultural revolution 83, 84

Daix, P. 54, 55, 56
Damnés de la Terre, Les 93, 94
Debray, R. 11, 85
Dedijer, V. 29
'Derniere Chance, La' 91
Desgraupes, P. 146
Diable et le bon dieu, Le 91
Dimitrov, G. 48, 50
Droit, M. 37
'Drole d'amitie', 44, 59
Dubuffet, J. 113
Duclos, J. 55, 56

Engrenage, L' 91
Entretiens sur la politique 89
Etre et le néant, L' xiii, 50, 91
existentialism 13, 51, 52, 83, 113, 114, 115, 116, 117, 122, 123, 124, 125, 144, 150
Existentialisme, L' 48, 53
Existentialisme est un humanisme, L' 91
Existentialisme n'est pas un humanisme, L' 52
Express, L' 26, 139

Fanon, F. 93, 94
'Fantôme de Staline, Le' 14, 91
Faurisson, R. 149
Fautrier, J. 113
Fifth Republic 12, 21, 26, 27, 33, 86, 88, 93
Figaro, Le 23, 97, 111, 139
Flaubert, G. xi, 87, 94, 132, 133
Force de l'age, La 121, 122
Fourth Republic 12, 14, 26, 28, 86, 92, 93
France Soir 134, 140, 141
Free French 23, 26
Freud, S. 29

Garaudy, R. 48, 50
Gauche Prolétarienne (GP) 67, 68, 76
Gaulle, C. de 7, 14, **17–39**, 66, 67, 77, 93, 94, 135, 139, 140, 144, 145, 146
Gaullism 3, 7, 12, 14, **17–39**, 52, 76, 94, 139, 144
Gavi, P. 36
Geismar, A. 79
General Agreement on Tariffs and Trade (GATT) 148
Genet, J. 117, 124, 132
Giacometti, A. 3, 85, 90, **113–32**
Gide, A. 85
Giraud, H. 24, 139
Giscard d'Estaing, V. 30, 34, 35, 147
Goebbels, J. 149
Goncourt, E. and J. 87
Gorz, A. 150
Graiavaka, O. 141
Gruber, F. 113

Haigh, A. 74
Heidegger, M. 52
Hélion, J. 113
Hervé, P. 145
Hitler, A. 25, 61, 144, 146
Humanité, L' 97, 98
Hungary 14, 52

Idiot de la famille, L' 94, 95
Idt, G. 44

J'Accuse 67, 94
Jambet, C. 72
Jean sans terre 38
Jeanson, H. 54
Jeux sont faits, Les 91
Jullian, M. 34, 147
July, S. 79

Kanapa, J. 50, 52, 54, 55
Kean 91
Khan, G. 137
Khrushchev, N. 66
Korean War 13, 52
Kravchenko affair 103

Lanzmann, C. 142, 148
Lazareff, P. 111, 134, 140, 141, 142

Le Bris, M. 75
Le Dantec, J.-P. 73, 75
Lecanuet, J. 30
Leclerc, G. 54
Lecoeur, A. 57, 60, 61
Lefebvre, H. 48, 50, 52, 53, 56
Lettres françaises, Les 49, 50, 57, 61, 97, 98
Levy, B. 38, 78, 79, 153
Liberation 18, 41, 43, 49, 61, 76
Libération 14, 34, 36, 67, 79, 94, 139, 140, 141, 142, 143, 145
liste noire 57

Macarthyism 109
Maier-Witt, S. 74
Mains sales, Les 91, 108
Malraux, A. 85
Manichaeism 63, 71
Maoism 3, 8, 12, 15, 16, 33, **63–79**, 143
Marcel, G. 109
Marcellin, R. 72, 76
Marshall Plan 28, 51, 52
Martin-Chauffier, L. 53
Marxism 43, 44, 50, 68, 92, 98
'Matérialisme et révolution' 50
Maulnier, T. 109
Mauriac, F. 116
May 1968 14, 16, 31, 32, 33, 67, 94, 99, 148, 153
Merleau-Ponty, M. 26, 41, 42, 45, 115
Michaux, H. 113
Miller, H. 51
Mitterrand, F. 148
Molotov, V. 46
Monde, Le 98
Morgan, C. 53, 61
Mort dans l'âme, La 44, 91
Mots, Les 93, 121, 124
Mur, Le 91
Murdoch, R. 134

Nausée, La 90, 91, 118
Nazi–Soviet pact 44, 46, 55, 56, 57, 58
Nekrassov 3, 89, 91, **97–112**, 141, 142
Nizan, H. 48, 55
Nizan, P. 1, 4, 10, 13, **41–61**, 68, 88, 92, 94
Nogrette, R. 72
Nouvel observateur, Le 31, 140
Nouvelle Résistance Prolétarienne (NRP) 72

Observer xii
Occupation 49, 55, 58, 76, 77, 87
On a raison de se révolter 36
Organisation de la Radio-Télévision Française (ORTF) 34, 35, 146
Orphée noir 91
Ortoli, F. 70
Orwell, G. 149
Overney, P. 72, 76

Parain, B. 54
Parti Communiste Français (PCF) 7, 8, 12, 13, 14, 15, 16, **41–61**, 68, 76, 92, 94, 98, 99, 109
'parti des fusillés, le' 49, 51, 57
Partito Communista Italiano (PCI) 68
Paulhan, J. 54, 57, 58, 59
'Peintures de Giacometti, Les' 128
Pétain, P. 24, 36, 139
Phoney War 57
Picasso, P. 113
Pierrard, A. 60
Poésie 47 54
Pompidou, G. 76, 145, 146
Pontalis, J.-B. 7, 16, 25
Popular Front 45
Pouillon, J. 58
'Présentation des *Temps Modernes*' 87

Qu'est-ce que la littérature? 52, 115

Ramadier, P. 51, 57, 144, 145
Rassemblement Démocratique Révolutionnaire (RGR) 13
Rassemblement du Peuple Français (RPF) 24, 25, 26
'Recherche de l'Absolu', La' 125
Red Army Faction 74
Réflexions sur la question juive 91
Resistance 52, 57, 58, 77
Ribbentrop, J. 46
Richier, G. 113
Rimbaud, A. 57, 58
Rolland, R. 54, 57, 58
Rondeau, D. 71
Rossi, A. 48, 56
Russell Tribunal 29, 30

Saint Genet, comédien et martyr 91, 118, 124
Sartre, J.-P.
comradeship 68
death 17
exemplary quality xiii, 3, 4
intellectual terrorist 116, 117, 123, 132
fellow-traveller 46, 50, 59
freedom of expression 35
funeral xi, 148
imperialism 42, 45, 58, 59, 116
libertarian 78
macho 45
Nobel Prize 138
prisoner of war 49
radicalism 4, 11, 15, 16, 33, 123
rootlessness 18, 37, 38, 39, 94
sectarian 45, 59, 66, 78
self-criticism 153
stabilising influence 79
totalitarian 45, 58, 116
traditional intellectual xi
women 43
Sartre Studies International xiv, xv
Schleyer, H.-M. 74
Schmidt, H. 74
Schuman, R. 144
Second World War 9, 19, 87, 92
Section Française de l'International Ouvrière (SFIO) 13
Seghers, P. 54
'Semence et le scaphandre, La' 44
Séquestrés d'Altona, Les 93, 101, 108
seriality 21, 22
Sicard, M. 118, 131
Siegel, L. 42, 72
Situations 89, 91, 93
Sorbonne 83, 85
Stalin, J. 149
Steiner, G. 49
surrealism 115, 116, 122, 123, 124, 131
Sursis, Le 90, 91

Tasca, A. 56
Tate Gallery xi, 113, 125, 132
Témoignage chrétien 98
Temps Modernes, Les 24, 25, 32, 35, 45, 50, 53, 60, 87, 125, 144
Téry, S. 48
Third Republic 10, 12, 86
Thorez, M. 47, 50, 51, 56, 57, 68
Tintoretto, J. xii, 119, 120
Titian, V. xii, 119, 120
Todd, O. xii, xiii, 115, 116, 117, 125, 132, 146
Togliatti, P. 68
Torres, H. 25, 32, 144
'Tribune des Temps Modernes, La' 144
Trotsky, L. 54
Troyennes, Les 93
Tynan, K. xii

Union des Démocrates pour la République (UDR) 22

United Kingdom Society for Sartrean Studies xiv

Valéry. P. 85
Van Velde, B. 113
Vichy 36, 56
Victor, P. 36
Vidéothèque de Paris 17, 38 39
Vietnam 14, 29, 30, 66, 93
violence **63–79**
'Visages' 120
Vivien, R.-A. 35, 36, 139, 147

Wolfromm, J.-D. 35
Wols, A. 113, 114, 115, 117, 120

Zhdanov, A. 50